TIPS AND TRICKS FOR A HEALTHY VAN LIFESTYLE

FROM WHEELS TO WELLNESS

Kristine Hudson

This guide is written from a combination of experience and high-level research. Even though we have done our best to ensure this book is accurate and up to date, there are no guarantees to the accuracy or completeness of the contents herein.

This book has been designed using resources from unsplash.com

ISBN 978-1-953714-27-5

Reviews

Reviews and feedback help improve this book and the author. If you enjoy this book, we would greatly appreciate it if you could take a few moments to share your opinion and post a review on Amazon.

Also by Kristine Hudson

Things Every Lifer Needs to Know

mybook.to/vanlife

Finding Success Outside The Traditional Office

mybook.to/workfromanywhere

How to Choose the Ultimate Side-hustle

mybook.to/side-hustle

The Modern Woman's Guide to Living Wild and Free

mybook.to/vanbundle1

Living and Prospering Wherever You Wish

mybook.to/vanbundle2

Contents

Section 1: Introduction

If you're reading this book, chances are pretty good that you're either knee-deep in van life or preparing to embark on the greatest adventure of your life. After all, the topic of maintaining your health and wellness while living on the road is a pretty niche topic.

But this book is intended not just for van lifers, but for roadtrippers, frequent fliers, and anyone whose lifestyle lacks routine, ordinariness, or regularity. This is the 21st century; technology has made a lot of previously unimaginable things very possible.

For example, living on the road is no longer for "hobos and nomads," as my grandmother was fond of saying. Van life is accessible to many people; it's become a way of life for more individuals than ever before. Whether they are living on the road full-time, or taking every possible opportunity to roam, more and more people are packing up their families, their pets, and their jobs to make a home on wheels.

It's not just the #VanLife crowd, either. While some like to "blame" the Millennial penchant for wanderlust for the sudden renewed interest in traveling to all ends of the Earth, the truth is that humans have always loved travel. Many of us are exercising this innate need to roam and choose to broaden our horizons by learning more about the places and people that make up this beautiful planet.

And so here you are, ready to immerse yourself in new experiences through previously uncharted territory. You've probably considered so many things and made so many decisions, but honestly, the process is just starting. A life on the road- whether a permanent situation or a small dose of freedom - requires making a lot of choices on the fly:

> "Do I stop for gas now, or hope I can make it to the next town?"
> "Should I take the loop trail clockwise or counter-clockwise?"
> "Can I fit in a three-mile bike ride before my next conference call?"

These questions are just a sample of the regular thoughts from any traveler's day.

Therefore, it stands to reason that some things are going to fall by the wayside. One of the most common things people forget when traveling – besides their toothpaste – is to take care of themselves physically, psychologically, and even preventively. It's really easy to get swept up in the day-to-day of just experiencing things, and forget about some of the more mundane aspects of existence.

When we live in a stationary home, we regularly get reminders about that sort of thing. The dentist sends a cheerful postcard to remind us to stop by. Doctors call to confirm your appointments 24 hours ahead of time. Commercials for your favorite brand of vitamins remind you to add them to the grocery list. There's a sense of order that comes with domesticity.

But then you hit the road. Days stop having names and numbers. It's a blur of places, things, experiences, and emotions, and you honestly can't remember what you had for dinner two nights ago, much less whether you took your vitamins. And are you squinting because of the sun, or because it's been two years since your last eye exam?

These things catch up with us quickly, and if there's one thing people on the road "ain't got time for," it's being out of commission due to illness or injury. From nasty viruses and mental malaise to breaks and sprains, it doesn't take much to take you out of the game when you're traveling.

I wrote this guide as a gentle reminder for everyone on the road to take care of themselves. If there's one thing we have learned during the COVID-19 crisis, it's that disease travels faster than we do. Despite anyone's best intentions, you can never be too cautious about health and wellness.

My van life journey started in 2018, before masks and social distancing became part of the experience. Even then, my husband Brad and I were surprised at how devastating even a simple cold could be to our lifestyle. To write this book, I've worked with other van lifers and folks within the health and medical communities – from nurses and pediatricians to physical therapists and nutritionists – who shared tips, experiences, and ideas related to maintaining your own wellness while doing some serious traveling.

While I can't promise that you'll live forever without a single sniffle after reading this book, I am fairly confident that you'll gain a few ideas that can help you improve your overall outlook on wellness. My goal is simply to point out some of the challenges that we might encounter on the road, in the wild, or anytime we abandon ourselves to a less domesticated lifestyle, and to equip you with a few pointers to confront those obstacles with practical solutions.

Whether you use this book as a launching pad for a daily health regimen or as a reminder to refill your first aid kit, consider the information in this book, as well as the resources at the end, as a reference for whenever you find yourself in a state of adventuring. After all, there's never a bad time to practice healthy habits!

Chapter 1: What You Need to Know

There are germs literally everywhere. I'm not telling you this because you don't know it. Companies that market cleaning products spend billions of dollars each year to make sure we all know it. I'm mentioning this here within the context of this book because all of the little particles of bacteria, viruses, molds, and fungi that you meet on a doorknob in New Orleans, at a gas station in Topeka, or even at a campsite in Colusa, are more than happy to move into your van and tag along on your adventures. Science moment: most bacteria and viruses don't live on surfaces as long as they do in a host because their ability to reproduce is compromised. However, there are always exceptions. A lot of rhinoviruses, one of the organisms behind the common cold, can remain on your hands in an infectious state for hours. Methicillin-resistant Staphylococcus aureus – better known by its street name, MRSA – can hang out on surfaces for weeks, just waiting for a nice open wound to start infecting your body.

Now, my goal here isn't to scare you into never leaving the van again. The point I'm trying to make is that there are different types of bacteria, viruses, molds, and fungi everywhere, and you're going to encounter them no matter what. When you live in a van or have a very travel-forward lifestyle, you're going to be taking your hands everywhere you go. They'll meet all sorts of new germs, and they may even be responsible for introducing new flora and fauna to new areas... if you don't take precautions.

Again, this isn't supposed to be scary, just a little bit of common-sense. You've probably been through this experience on a smaller scale whenever you start a new job, your child returns to school, or you take the whole family on a vacation; within a week or two, everyone in your household gets sick with the same thing. It's very common though, and usually not devastating. Your body getting sick is how it trains itself to make antibodies that protect you the next time you encounter that particular strain of germ.

As travelers, we live by the phrase "take nothing but pictures; leave nothing but footprints." So, we're automatically responsible for not starting a wave of infection in the places we visit. Many indigenous people were wiped out when new diseases were brought to their homelands. Even though the difference between Indiana and Iowa today may not seem great, the idea of getting an entire community sick because we happened to stop at a gas station at the same time is more guilt than I personally can handle.

The magnitude of our impact is more than we can measure, so as van lifers, we need to be aware of our own actions. Not just for the health and wellness of everyone in our van, but for the communities we visit too.

In this book, we'll look at ways to nurture a healthy lifestyle in and out of the van. I am not going to give you diet ideas or weight loss or weight training tips. I'm not going to tell you what combination of essential oils will cure dysentery. What I am going to do is remind you of all the things that might fall by the wayside when you leave domesticity behind. If the last few paragraphs have had any impact on you, you shouldn't be surprised when I say the number one thing you need to do on the road, no matter what, is **wash your hands!**

Let's expand on that. Let's take a look at not just how you can reduce the spread of disease, but how you can take care of yourself no matter where you are. Everything from preventive care to keep yourself well, to supplies every van lifer should have on hand, to nutrition and exercise tips, mental health considerations, and even what you can do to reduce your own germy footprints will make an appearance in the following pages.

Consider this book a handy helper to remind you to take care of yourself no matter where you're going. If you haven't left the stationary home yet, some of this might seem obvious. But once you answer the call of the wild and hit the road, you may find that you become a bit... well, feral, for lack of a better term. My goal is to create a few "oh yeah" moments to keep your mind and body on track for staying healthy no matter what sort of shenanigans you're enjoying!

Chapter 2: What Do I Know?

So if I'm writing a book about health and wellness, I must be a doctor, right? I'm not. Though I worked in close proximity with doctors for years as a human resources consultant within the health and wellness division of an insurance company, that hardly counts as medical credentials.

An amusing truth is that everyone in my family is either a healthcare worker or an engineer. I'm the "black sheep" writer, but this actually works in my favor. Whenever something stops working correctly – whether it's me or something in my home – I have someone to call. And whenever they need their resumes updated, they call me. It's a reciprocal relationship!

When I was packing for my first van excursion, I had a panel of experts to explain exactly why I needed to pack acetaminophen, ibuprofen, and naproxen (it has to do with the way each provides relief for fevers and inflammation, if you're wondering). Not everyone has access to that type of support, so I wanted to share what I could, when I could, to help any other van newbies who are standing in similar shoes, wondering what's enough.

Two years on the road leaves you with plenty of experiential knowledge too. I'm not here to share weird tips and tricks that may or may not be medically sound, but practical things you wish someone would tell you. Like, "pack way more towels than you think you need." Think of this book as a favorite uncle, giving you a few pointers from hard-earned experience.

While not all of the advice in this book is anecdotal, I am going to tell quite a few stories. One thing that I did not fully realize until I started living in a van is that I am clumsy. I lack balance, grace, and coordination on an almost amusing level. As a result, many of the things I have learned about keeping the body well come from orthopedists, sports physicians, and physical therapists I've met along the way. These trained professionals have listened to my complaints and helped me come up with van-friendly ways to keep my battered body functioning, despite my best efforts. I'm not trying to take the place of these experts, but instead share what they wish they could tell everyone in my shoes.

The topic of mental health is also near and dear to me. Like many people in the United States, I struggle with anxiety and depression. This is something I have been working on since I first came into the realization that I was not okay in 1999. I'm not an expert, just someone who is acutely aware of how being on the road can do strange things to not just your body, but your mind. The section about mental health isn't just going to be a list of what I do, but more of a collection of recommendations I've learned from working very closely with mental healthcare providers and others on the road.

If you are ready for help right now, here are some immediate resources:
-   The 24/7 helpline for Substance Abuse and Mental Health Services

Administration is 1-800-662-HELP (4357).
- Lifeline for National Suicide Prevention can be reached at 1-800-273-8255.

Both of these numbers provide free, confidential connection to individuals and services that can help you. You can also find more information in the Resources section.

Finally, I don't want anyone to think that I'm a health snob or a wellness know-it-all. I have never had a kale smoothie, and I sometimes forget my sunblock. If anything, think of this book as a good friend or worldly relative coming up to you before you leave for the road and saying, "Hey, let me tell you about a bunch of stuff I didn't think of. Here's how they came to be a problem, and here's what I learned about it." Take what you will. I'm not going to make medical recommendations. I am going to share stories about the cringe-worthy lessons my husband and I have learned about health and wellness on the open road. I'm definitely going to tell you about the time I fell off a cliff (and hopefully you'll laugh as much as I did).

Don't consider this book a byway for actual medical advice. I'm not diagnosing anything or recommending a course of treatment. I am, however, going to tell you to wash your hands; in fact, I'll mention it frequently. And while you're at it, your laundry, your van, your produce, and... well, just read on.

Section 2: Taking Care of Your One and Only Body

You've probably heard the phrase "You've only got one body!" While it's typically thrown about in an annoying diet campaign, there's no denying the truth of the statement. In fact, there's nothing that validates the phrase quite like choosing to live a nomadic lifestyle in a van.

At least, that's what was running through my mind when I battled a fever and tonsillitis somewhere in Upstate New York. Our first tour of the United States was winding down, and I was torn between trying to power through hiking the Adirondacks or sleeping until I felt better. I felt so crummy, I actually cried. I desperately wanted to feel great and do all the things I dreamed of doing. "I may never get this chance again!" my brain wailed. "Yes, but you've only got one body," shot back my throat, raging with infection.

I share this experience because we're often very stubborn when it comes to our overall physical health. Most of us know how to eat well, brush our teeth, and exercise regularly. These are all great habits to maintain and will do a lot to keep you healthy in the long run. But let's take a few things out of the equation. For example, let's say you have limited access to running water. You have no idea where the closest grocery store is. You have extremely limited refrigeration, and there's definitely not a treadmill in sight.

Van life is full of sacrifices – many of which are made gleefully – but your health should not be one of the choices on the table. You may not have considered the impact of van life on seemingly insignificant activities like brushing your teeth. However, it only takes one day without running water to realize how much we take these things for granted. Even the act of getting up at midnight for a quick trip to the bathroom can become challenging when your home has four wheels (and no toilet).

So, let's take a look at some of the things you can do to proactively keep that one and only magnificent body of yours in top condition while on the road. You may still miss some of the convenience of having a stationary kitchen and bathroom, but you don't have to sacrifice overall wellness!

Chapter 1: Keeping Up with Preventive Care

Preventive care is an umbrella term for taking care of your body each and every day to prevent future illnesses. The concept is obvious: if you take care of your body, you will be rewarded with wellness. Granted, preventive care isn't going to take care of every possibility. The human body is vast, complex, and does a lot of weird things when we least expect it. Just as you have packed your van to be prepared for whatever comes your way, practicing regular preventive care is the best way to do the same for your body.

The following preventive care guidelines are all equally important, so please don't view this as a definitive ranking of what to do. Instead, consider all of these as reminders that even though you're living a "wild and free" lifestyle, every body has limitations.

The Steps to Preventive Care

The first recommendation I'd like to share is to **Get Checked Out.** While no one understands the experience of living in your body as well as you do, you can easily be unaware of some of the finer details of your existence. Therefore, it's a great idea to visit a general practitioner, dentist, and optometrist (eye-doctor) on a regular basis.

I know what you're thinking, believe me. No one really enjoys going for a physical or dental exam. It's time-consuming, it almost always results in bad news and anxiety, it's expensive, and in some cases, painful. Even if the doctor helpfully offers a lollipop after everything is said and done, our adult brains aren't sure that what we've endured was worth it.

The truth is that regular examinations are one of the simplest ways to maintain good health. When you go in for a standard physical, your doctor will check your weight, blood pressure, and check your breathing and heart rate. They may also run some biometric blood work to measure cholesterol, and blood sugar. While this may seem like a giant waste of time to people who are regularly active and in good health, here's the bottom line: **most of the time, we don't know what's wrong unless we know what's right.**

By receiving regular physical examinations, you'll get to know your baseline levels – what "healthy" looks like for your body. That way, when something does feel bad, you'll be able to compare it to what "good" feels like for you.

Additionally, visiting a doctor regularly provides the opportunity to find early warning signs of potential health problems. The more data you have regarding your own health, the easier it will be to catch any inconsistencies that could become a much larger obstacle down the road.

The same goes for dental exams. Practicing regular dental health is relatively simple, even in a van. We'll dive into some additional tips on how to work oral hygiene into a world without running water later in this book, but brushing and flossing regularly is the first step in keeping your teeth and gums healthy. It's also a great idea to visit a dentist at least once a year to thoroughly check for cavities, signs of disease, and other problems that you might not be able to see or diagnose on your own.

Last, but certainly not least, are eye exams. Millions of people around the world rely on corrective lenses of some sort. Contrary to the teasing we may have received in elementary school, wearing glasses is a fantastic idea for those with less than perfect vision. Straining to see properly can cause a lot of wear and tear on the eyes and result in some pretty mind-blowing headaches.

Let's not be coy. If you're driving a van, you really should have your eyes checked for the safety of your passengers and everyone else on the road. Driving with impaired vision is really dangerous. From an adventurer's point of view, why on Earth would you want to explore the planet if you can barely see it?

So, when should you visit all of these medical practitioners? Well, experts don't entirely agree on frequency, but "at least once a year" seems to be the consensus. Younger people with low family history of risk or no pre-existing conditions can often get away with having a physical every three years. Children, those over 50, and anyone experiencing chronic conditions should visit more frequently.

Other wellness exams that are dependent on age, sex, and family history are also recommended. For example, all women should receive a Well Woman visit each year, and women over 40 should receive regular mammograms. Colonoscopies are recommended for adults over 50 or those with a family history of digestive tract issues.

In many cases, I might be preaching to the proverbial choir here. You might be well on board with preventive care, but you may simultaneously wonder how you're supposed to do all that from a van, RV, skoolie, or another free-wheeling home base.

There are a few options in this modern world! One rather recent advent is the walk-in clinic model. These walk-in style operations can be found in grocery stores and pharmacies, or as free-standing options for those who need simple and direct medical care. Often, you can visit any of these at any time during their open hours without an appointment or by calling ahead. They provide a variety of services, such as physical exams, vaccinations, and consultations. Generally speaking, you'll be in and out from your session very quickly, and at a low cost.

Surprisingly, vision exams can also be very simply arranged. Reputable eye care resources can be found in department stores and shopping malls. While eye appointments may need to be scheduled in advance, it's generally quite simple to find a nearby practice with an appointment available when scrolling through a quick online search via your smartphone.

Dental care can be a bit trickier because appointments tend to fill up quickly and may be hard to come by, unless you have a true dental emergency. If you have a dentist you know and love, you may wish to finagle your road trip so that you'll be in the neighborhood. This is actually my preferred method, because Brad and I are really, really bad about going to the dentist regularly. Brad just never got in the habit of going each year, and

I have an active terror of dentists (my apologies to anyone in the dental community- it's not you, it's me!). We found a patient and thorough dentist at our home base in Ohio. When we get our reminder texts from the practice, we make appointments, then get ready to loop back home for a few weeks. We get the opportunity to visit with our friends and family at home, and take care of that annual dentist visit in one swoop. In our case, we also throw in any other yearly check-ups as well.

Another option is to "plant" for a bit. In this case, you find a place to park for a few weeks and schedule any and all appointments to coincide with your time at that location. This can be helpful for any appointments that may have a potential follow-up, regardless of the type of practitioner you see. I have seen many traveling families utilize this option to ensure all the kids are able to see the doctor, dentist, and optometrist at once. Especially in cases where a doctor may have to order out for a prescription (or in the case of vision, order contacts or glasses for you), it can be easier to stay in one place for a bit. While some van dwellers may wince at the idea of staying in place for more than a few nights, remember this sacrifice is ultimately for your health and longevity!

Hand-in-hand with getting regular check-ups as part of your preventive care routine is vaccinations and booster shots. I know this is a super controversial topic, and I'm not going to spend time fanning the flames with discussion about whether you should or should not be vaccinated. I'll assume that, if you're reading this book, you are a grown adult with bodily autonomy who can make those decisions for yourself. If you are making decisions on behalf of your children, I hope that you do so with a full understanding of your family members' health and well-being.

I would also like to mention that a nomadic lifestyle has its own perils when it comes to spreading and contracting disease, as we van lifers come in contact with more people and more potential health threats than most people. Instead, we spend all of our time in an incubator on wheels, dragging all the fun viruses and bacteria we encounter along the way back to our van. While this book is filled with tips that can help mitigate becoming a modern day Typhoid Mary, there is significant scientific data that suggests that certain vaccines will help in this regard as well.

Additionally, if this is your first time living largely in the wilderness, you may want to consider potential environmental concerns that can be avoided with vaccinations. Clostridium bacteria, which causes Tetanus, are common in soil, dust, and manure deposits, all of which are very commonly found in the wilderness. This bacteria enters the body through even small cuts and impacts the central nervous system. Ultimately, untreated tetanus can lead to death by suffocation as muscles spasm and harden throughout the body.

Another consideration is rabies. Wild animals all over the United States can become infected by and transmit rabies, even though encountering a rabid animal in cities and suburbs is far less likely. When you're on the trail or boondocking, however, it's highly unlikely that an Animal Control official will roll up at exactly the right time to capture and remove the suffering animal. Instead, the best idea is to not come in direct contact with any wild animal you meet along the way, and consider getting a rabies vaccine before you hit the road.

Next on the preventive care checklist are your maintenance medications. Nearly half the population requires a daily dose of some type of medication, so if this is you, you're not alone. "Maintenance medication" refers to daily medication required for chronic conditions such as diabetes, asthma, arthritis, and many more.

The reason these drugs are so effective at helping people maintain wellness is because they are taken every day. This means a consistent amount of the drug is present to relieve certain symptoms. Without these drugs, individuals can experience a great deal of discomfort or potential-ly life-threatening symptoms. Therefore, it is important that anyone on a maintenance medication stay on a regular schedule.

There are two components to this: scheduling and refilling. Many of these drugs must be taken at the same time each day, while others need to be taken as symptoms present themselves. If you are on a daily schedule, there's one little, sneaky thing that happens as you travel – time zones. If you'll be going back and forth across time zones, make sure you discuss this with your doctor to avoid any unpleasant situations.

The thought of refilling your prescriptions while on the road can be intimidating. Personally, I'm on several daily medications for a slew of conditions, and I was genuinely afraid that I would have to return to Ohio every month to pick up my drugs. One of my doctors was an invaluable resource; she made sure I transferred all of my prescriptions to a national pharmacy chain. She also put a note on the prescription file that could be viewed through the pharmacy's system, explaining that I am traveling, and if I request my prescriptions in another state, it is valid. There were very few instances in which I wasn't able to waltz into the local chain and pick up my prescription. However, in those cases, the pharmacy staff very helpfully contacted my doctor, who was able to verify my prescription. All I had to do was present identification!

In many ways, picking up meds on the road was easier than at home. Many national chains have mobile apps, which help you find local pharmacies and request refills to specific locations. Just make sure you opt out of any automatic refills, or your prescription might be waiting for you to pick up several states away!

A Few Words About Insurance

The American concept of health, dental, and vision insurance is incredibly complicated. I should know – employee benefits was my area of expertise during my 10+ years in human resources. The concept is so complicated, in fact, I was hired as a personalized coach to explain health and welfare benefits to their employees. My main takeaway from that project was that health insurance has become nearly impossible for the everyday person to understand.

And to make matters worse, it's equally as difficult to survive in this country without health insurance. My goal is not to make this a whiny rant, but the facts speak for themselves. As a clumsy person, I once managed to slice my hand open while opening a $1 dog toy. What can I say? I'm talented. The resulting emergency room visit consisted of a nurse practitioner evaluating the wound, determining it could not be stitched due to its placement, giving me a special soap to keep it clean, and showing me how to bandage it to minimize the scar. As I was without insurance at the time, the visit resulted in a $1250 bill.

Naturally, I immediately regretted seeking medical attention. Amusingly enough, for my troubles of having to choose between paying rent and a medical bill for a few months, I still have no feeling in part of my finger. At least the scar is kind of cute!

Medical care is incredibly expensive. Health insurance is also very expensive, and incredibly confusing. So, what should you do?

My number one recommendation is to do the math. There are a lot of factors that go into determining whether or not you should have health insurance, and from there, what type of plan you should have.

First, consider your overall budget. What type of income will you be looking at in your van life scenario? Do you have a savings or checking account as a safety net?

Next, consider your overall health. Do you have any chronic conditions? Do you require maintenance prescriptions? Are you relatively healthy, but accident prone? One small detour to take in these considerations is to note what you plan to do while living in your van, and any potentially related risks to your health. Are you going to spend a lot of time driving, which could increase your chances of being in an automobile-related accident? Will you be doing a lot of hiking, climbing, or rappelling? Those are more risk factors to take into consideration.

A typical emergency room visit costs upwards of $1,000 without insurance, and visits to urgent care are generally in the low $100s to low $1,000s, depending on your reason for visiting. My visit to urgent care for having debris removed from my ear was around $300 without insurance. However, going to the emergency room after hours to assess my injuries after falling off of a cliff would have been around $8,000 without insurance. I meant it when I said I was accident prone – Brad and I actually accounted for me to have two medical emergencies each year when doing this exercise ourselves.

What we're gathering here are the numbers of "What You Can Afford" and "Anticipated Medical Costs." If you're pretty healthy, but your chances of falling off a cliff as I did are high, then you might want to include up to $10,000 for medical expenses. I got off lightly because I have my own crutches and air cast.

If you have regular prescriptions you must take, check out the price before and after insurance, if you're purchasing them with insurance right now. If you have regular medical appointments, add those to the total based on the rate you are currently billed AND what they would cost if you didn't have insurance.

You might benefit from making an easy chart like this:

Expense	With Insurance	Without Insurance
Daily Prescriptions	$35/month = $420 total	$550/month = $6,600 total
Appointment with Dr. Smith	$20 copay per visit x 4 visits per year $80 total	$165 per visit x 4 visits per year $660 total
Potential visit to urgent care (hypothetical)	$75 copay	$500
Total Costs	$420 + $80 + $75 = $575	$6,600 + $660 + $500 = $7,650

The annual total with insurance is calculated as:

$35 x 12= $420

$20 x 4 = $80

$420 + $80 + $75 = $575

We use the same process for the "without insurance" figures:

$550 x 12 = $6,600

$165 x 4 = $660

$6,600 + $660 + $500= $7,760

These numbers are actually based on my own medical usage, using my current insurance for the "with insurance" figures, and my experiences without insurance in 2017 for the "without insurance" figures. Your own expenses may vary greatly, so don't necessarily copy my work here!

So, you may be thinking that I just made a very compelling case for insurance, but don't act too quickly! We haven't gotten through all of the expenses!

The next thing to consider is how much health insurance costs. If you're lucky enough to have an employer who doesn't mind that you work on the road and will provide employee health benefits automatically deducted from your paycheck, this should be a slam dunk obvious decision. However, not all of us have those resources. Brad and I have only had access to employer-sponsored healthcare in the last year. Prior to that, we self-paid at the contracted company rate. *Prior to that*, we were both on COBRA, which is a continuation of your employer-sponsored healthcare, at 100% of the market rate, plus an administration fee.

The national average cost for an independent health plan in 2020 is around $462 per month, but that cost depends greatly on your location, age, and tobacco use. Some independent plans require a health exam as well.

So, let's use the national average to determine what your annual healthcare coverage cost would be:

$462 for an independent monthly health plan x 12 months = $5,544 for annual health insurance

Add that to your medical expenses:

$5,544 for annual health insurance + $575 for annual health expenses with insurance) = $6,119 in medical expenses with health insurance

It's not quite as much of an obvious decision now, is it? If that hypothetical urgent care visit happens, having insurance and not having insurance is just a few hundred dollars different in annual expenses.

That being said, I also recommend looking into the options that are available to you. There are plans and subsidies available for those with minimal medical expenses that are much more affordable and can help with any unexpected and urgent expenses.

Additionally, if you have small children, I encourage you to do the math for each member of your family so you can gain a clear perspective on your healthcare needs as a family. If you or a little one takes after me and finds new and exciting ways to fall off of things, it might be worth it in the long run!

When choosing a plan, be sure to look at phrases like "copay," "deductible," "coinsurance," and "out of pocket maximum." Let's take a closer look:

1. Copay: This is a payment that you make each time you receive a specific service, whether that's a visit to a doctor or a prescription. Copays do not count towards your deductible, they come right out of your pocket and are typically paid directly to the provider (meaning, at the doctor's office or pharmacy, at the time of service).
2. Deductible: This is how much you have to pay each year before your medical plan starts paying co-insurance. Everything up to the limit of the deductible will be paid out of your pocket.

3. Coinsurance: Once you've paid your deductible, you and your insurance will split the bill for your medical services. You may see something like, "80% coinsurance after deductible." That means that your plan will pay 80% of each expense, and you'll pay 20%.

4. Out-of-Pocket Maximum: This is the most you will have to pay for your part of the coinsurance agreement. So, if you're paying 20% of each expense, those payments may eventually add up to the Out-of-Pocket Maximum. Once you've paid that amount, your plan will pay 100% of all expenses to the Lifetime Plan Maximum.

As much as I would love to teach a master class on understanding insurance plans again, I'll save that for another author or another book. In short, all of these numbers should be considered when evaluating your need for health insurance. I strongly urge anyone who is considering shopping for an individual or independent health plan to look at a document known as the "Summary Plan Description." This will help you carefully consider what is covered and how it is covered. For example, while my appointments with Dr. Smith, the general practitioner, have a very reasonable $20 copay, my appointments with Dr. Nelle, the chiropractor, are subject to the deductible and cost $40 each… unless I'm coming in for adjustments following an accident, and then those are subject to a $30 copay.

On top of that, you'll need to look at whether or not the plan has a national network of providers, meaning that you can receive medical coverage no matter where you and your van travel. Some plans offer Out-of-Network coverage at a higher deductible and lower coinsurance rate, so you'll want to be sure to visit only in-network providers whenever possible. Thankfully, it's pretty easy to research the network from each plan's customer website, or by contacting customer service.

It's enough to make the mind spin!

There's less to say about dental and vision insurance, since these types of coverages tend to be more straightforward. However, one thing to note when looking at these coverages is the plan's annual maximum, if any.

Some types of coverage do have a limit on what they'll cover in a year, so if you have a large dental emergency while on the road, you might be looking at a large bill. Additionally, most vision plans provide a free examination and an allowance on glasses or contacts, so depending on your vision needs, this may not even be worth the expense.

In conclusion, your choice to carry or not carry medical insurance really depends on whether or not it makes financial sense for your particular situation. I sincerely urge anyone to really take the time to do the math – ALL of the math – if this is a question in your mind.

Chapter 2: Nutrition and Eating for You

Food and eating are tricky in a van. I'm not just talking about how hard it is to balance a burrito on the steering wheel while you're cruising down the highway, either. I mean that many humans are pretty domesticated when it comes to food, food storage, and cooking. When you aren't going to the grocery store regularly to fill your beautiful refrigerator and freezer with fresh ingredients, when you don't have your choice from a handful of stirring utensils, and when there's no option to plant a garden each summer, you have to become inventive.

What's the first thing you do when you're going on a road trip? For most of us, it's a stop to the gas station where we fill up the tank, and then run inside for a whole bunch of snacks! Big, sugary, caffeinated drinks to keep us awake when the road becomes monotonous, and a whole bunch of delicious junk food that we can ONLY get at gas stations quickly fill the cup holders and seats, preparing to fuel the humans in the vehicle for the adventure ahead.

When I asked around amongst my kindred van lifers about health and wellness on the road, literally the first thing everyone mentioned was reducing junk food intake. This makes sense; after all, the temptation to abandon all nutrition is incredibly high when you live on the road. There will be stretches of road where your only options for caloric intake will be found at gas stations and fast-food drive-thrus. There will be even more times when the only options for sustenance are things that can be found in your van.

Furthermore, if you have a full day of driving planned, snacking is one way to take the boredom out of long, flat stretches of road where the scenery looks the same for miles and miles. Eating not only releases endorphins, which are a nice change of pace for a stagnant brain, but also gives you something to think about besides the monotony. Staring at the scrub brush flatlands of southern Texas made me so anxious for a change of scenery that I drank an entire liter of Topo Chico to wash down a giant concha I bought at a gas station. I have no regrets about the concha - it was handmade and delicious - but I can't tell you if I was actually hungry, or just ready to occupy my senses with something other than scrub and highway heat mirages.

Personally, I think that sampling a community's cuisine is an important part of learning about the culture. I'm incredibly inspired by Anthony Bourdain, Andrew Zimmern, and Samantha Brown, and their anthropological approach to food as a huge part of a cultural experience. I would encourage anyone who is traveling in new places to try every new flavor, texture, and ingredient they can get their hands on, because food is an incredible expression of who we are as people.

That being said, our bodies aren't designed to run exclusively on high fat, high salt, high sugar diets. As my friend and fellow van dweller Katie is fond of saying, "You've got to run a vegetable through the system once in a while." Thankfully, there are more and more nutritious items that can be found easily. From packages of raw carrots and other veggies to low-fat, vegan, and gluten-free snack options that offer vitamins, fiber, and protein. Snack culture is catching up with the needs of nutrition.

Nutrition isn't just some big hoax brought to us by Big Diet Culture. The body does need a certain amount of vitamins and minerals to oper-ate properly. From the digestive system to maintaining brain function, eating delivers the chemicals our body requires to live and thrive. The consequences of poor nutrition aren't that great, either- constipation, diarrhea, heartburn, fatigue, poor concentration, muscle weakness and dizziness... None of these symptoms are helpful for those who need to be on the road for long hours.

Therefore, eating on the road becomes a delicate balance of trying new things, while still being sure to get those fruits and veggies in, and keep regular salt, sugar, and fat intake at reasonable levels.

Another consideration in nutritional maintenance? Remembering to eat. When I lived in a house and worked in an office, the cues were always there to eat. Around noon, everyone starts heading out for lunch. Around 3pm, the afternoon doldrums creep in and it's time for a snack. After work, everyone wants dinner and bed. Radio and television commercials are specifically timed to get you thinking about your appetite. Even social media ads for food products are perfectly timed to coincide with meal times!

When you live in a van, far from the radio or the television, you don't get these prompts. Thankfully, someone had installed a CD player in our van before it came into our lives, but there was no AUX jack for streaming, no Bluetooth... in fact, not all of the speakers even worked. You don't realize how out of touch you are until you end up splurging on a hotel for the night and become absolutely entranced with commercials. Without social cues to eat, there were many days when, after morning caffeine, Brad and I would watch the sun setting on the road ahead of us and ask each other if we had eaten that day. Van life can literally be feast or famine.

Therefore, the first rules of van nutrition are as follows:
1. Experience culture through food
2. Nutrition is important
3. Remember to eat (and not always junk food!)

The Importance of Proper Food Storage

You might be thinking, "That's great, Kristine, but where am I getting all of these nutritious ingredients, and where am I putting them?" If there is one area in which van life is frustrating, it's definitely in the kitchen area.

If you have designed your van or skoolie with a functioning refrigerator and running water, you have made an excellent investment towards your health and wellness. In fact, when I broached the topic of food storage with other van dwellers, they literally could not fathom not having at least a refrigerator. Be it known, you do not need a refrigerator in order to be a legitimate van lifer who cares about their health and nutrition.

On our first time out, Brad and I didn't plan on having perishable goods. There was just no room for storing things that needed to be chilled, so we packed lots of high-quality low-sodium canned veggies, and whenever possible, bought local produce in small quantities that we could eat in one sitting. That, of course, brought on its own problems, because then we had to use our limited water supply to prepare veggies, and we felt incredibly guilty if we weren't able to eat it all.

We remedied this with a cooler that requires ice. Without a power supply, that was really the only option we had. And, as a bonus, the cooler could double as a seat, and the melted ice became cool, refreshing bathwater in the desert.

The problem with a cooler is that you really have to be on the beam at all times. For example, anything you place in a cooler must be in a water-tight container. Otherwise, the container will fill with water as the ice melts, and eventually, enough sloshing around will jar the contents of the container loose, filling your cooler with really wet hummus and cheese, for example. So far, the only way we have found to remove really pungent odors from a cooler is a blasting from a do-it-yourself car wash hose and a liberal application of Dawn dish soap.

Therefore, if you're going to use a cooler, I strongly recommend bringing along a full set of water-tight reusable containers, and transferring any fresh perishable food to the container immediately. By "immediately," I mean, "in the parking lot of the grocery store or market." This tends to be the easiest place to get things done because you're parked and have a place to dispose of the wrappers and original containers once you've placed everything safely in their new vessels.

The next tip for keeping a functioning cooler is to try as hard as possible to keep up with the ice levels. While having a bit of water for a bird bath is a great idea, a cooler full of tepid water is a huge temptation for bugs and smells bad. Also, most cold food is intended to remain cold, and as the temperature rises, the breeding of bad bacteria begins, creating the perfect storm of food poisoning. No one has time for this, especially if they live in a home on wheels.

I noticed that there are plenty of free-standing ice stations across the southern United States, especially in areas where fishing and hunting are very popular. These are great resources for van people, as you can generally park nearby and attend to your cooler situation in detail. Of course, most gas stations and grocery stores also sell ice, and it's relatively inexpensive.

Unfortunately, ice isn't one of those things you can just buy extra of- you can only put so much in the cooler, and then the rest melts. To offset this expense, I recommend purchasing drinking water quality ice and filling your water bottles with any excess ice that won't fit in the cooler. Excess ice can always be used somewhere. It can also be placed in spray bottles for spritz baths, saved for bathing and dishes, or incorporated into your toilet set up.

The next dilemma is keeping bugs and critters away from your food. Flies are going to be everywhere. Even if you have fantastic window screens and an amazing central air system in your van, the next time you open a door, flies, mosquitoes, and gnats are going to take advantage of the invitation to check out the inside of your awesome van. Spiders and centipedes (and worst of all- desert millipedes) will find a way in through some tiny, impossible hole somewhere. Smaller animals can slither up through the motor and make their way through the maze to the cabin. Once they're inside, the feast is on!

Your cooler and your refrigerator will typically have a seal that makes them impenetrable to insects and small animals, so we'll focus the attention of these endeavors on your dry goods. Cans are generally not a problem, either - they're not interesting. But any cardboard boxes or bags that you may have lying about are fair game.

I strongly recommend placing food items inside a tough rubber tote, particularly one that locks. These bins are smell-proof, which means they won't draw bears, coyotes, and raccoons to your van, and they are tight enough to prevent even the smallest flying creature from digging in. You can use a medium-sized tote for long term food storage, and smaller versions for your day-to-day snacks, or things you might wish to access from the front of the van.

Another great solution for storing dry food is plastic drawers. You may have built in a beautiful wooden cabinet in your van, and I commend you for doing so. However, if you store food in them, there are many small creatures in the wild with teeth that are made for gnawing through that gorgeous wooden patina. Additionally, these types of drawers and cabinets don't have the air-tight seal of a rubber bin, and insects will thrive in a bag of unattended crackers or cereal.

Anything airtight with a closing, locking lid should be sufficient. I've even seen some creative souls use large canisters and jars for storing various dry ingredients. My only caution is to make sure you have a way of securing those jars in transit, or your noggin might meet an unpleasant surprise the next time you open a cabinet or drawer.

Again, if you have the ability to transfer everything to a container that can be fully sealed, you'll be much better off. Does this take some of the spontaneity out of grocery shopping? Yes. Does this mean you have to be more mindful of your food levels? Absolutely. Will you find some food turning stale or going off before you can finish it? Unfortunately, yes, especially if you're a one or two-person van outfit.

One of the challenges of buying food for a nomadic lifestyle is that you have to be prepared to use it in many different ways. The carrots that you had for a snack earlier can be added to the stir fry you make later tonight. The lettuce from last night's salad can be the basis for today's sandwich. Whatever food products you buy, you have to be prepared to eat them right away, and until they're gone. Generally speaking, you can get two meals out of produce, one or two out of dairy products, and meat is best eaten immediately. If you have a high-powered refrigerator or freezer, these limits can be extended. Additionally, block cheese travels surprisingly well, as long as it doesn't get wet!

When you shop for food in a stationary home, you generally stock up for the week, or even the month. There are a lot of impulse purchases and ingredients bought for one specific meal or dish. In a van, even with a refrigerator, it's not quite that simple. Camper fridges are much smaller than the one you have at home, for starters, and require a significant amount of power to run appropriately. You're not going to have a bowl of fruit on the counter for folks to grab as they walk by, because that will turn into a Tim Burton-esque masterpiece of infestation very quickly. You probably won't be able to stock five different types of yogurt, and leftovers are going to be an exercise in delicacy and deliberation, between storage and reheating them. Bread can be tricky, too, as more humid areas will turn a loaf into a moldy garden almost immediately. Everything edible will need to be carefully considered before it enters the van, or your waste will quickly add up.

Based on all of this information, you may be pretty convinced that cooking a healthful meal while living in a van is pretty much impossible. Somewhere in your camping psyche, you may be stuck on traditional campfire meals, such as hot dogs diligently roasted on sticks, beans cooked in a can, and the sticky, crunchy delight of a sweet s'mores treat.

While you can absolutely indulge in what Brad and I call "The Campsite Classic" from time to time, eating hot dogs every meal, every day, for any length of time is probably appealing to only the most discerning toddler. It's also not exactly nutritionally balanced.

One of the best investments any hard-core camper, van lifer, or boondocker can make is a portable propane burner. Most versions are small, which trans-lates to "travels well." They're easy to find at home improvement stores, hardware stores, or places that sell camping goods.

These small burners typically require an equally tiny propane tank, typically sold at the same location as the burner. While having equipment that is small in size is wonderful for stashing it in the compromised living quarters of a van, it also means that you'll only get so many meals out of each tank. Therefore, you'll likely want to have more than one on hand at all times. You'll also need to be conscious of how long it takes to make meals.

Another factor in the space vs. time vs. nutrition trifecta is your kitchenware. It may be tempting to pack up all of your cookware, especially if you're very experienced and adept in the kitchen; the truth is that you can get away with a very minimal list of supplies and still have everything you need to eat well every day.

If you've read any of my other van books, you'll know that Brad and I have compartmentalized everything that would be a "room" into a heavy-duty tote of its own. His office, which consists of a gazebo-style tent, folding table, and folding chair, along with his minimalistic approach to office supplies, takes up one tote. We have an emergency tote, which includes jumper cables, a tire changing kit, road flares, first aid kits (yes, plural. We'll talk about those in a minute), tarp, bungee cable tie-downs, funnels, a tool kit, and related mechanical supplies in another tote. Our bed linens have their own smaller tote, while the laundry has a bag within a tote.

The kitchen, therefore, has its own tote, which is surprisingly smaller than you would imagine. Our burner actually came in its own housing, so it lives on its own behind the driver's seat. The propane tanks are in the tote, along with the following:

- One 3-quart pot
- A cast iron skillet
- Three forks, three spoons, two steak knives
- One multi-function can opener
- One spatula and one non-slotted cooking spoon
- Two large plates
- Two large bowls
- Two each dish rags and dish towels
- One dishpan
- One small bottle of environmentally friendly dish soap

The rest of the room in this particular tote is devoted to canned and dry goods for several reasons. First, canned soup, tuna, pasta, peanut butter, beans, and instant rice are all great staples to have on-hand for an actual rainy day. They heat up quickly without draining the propane, and with little mess or fuss. Second, refer back to the part where we keep our dry goods locked up to prevent infestation. Cans aren't in as much danger, obviously, but keeping everything centralized makes it so much easier. Lastly, the weight of the cans prevents the tote from shifting too much while we drive. That means we can strategically stack it next to a lighter or currently empty tote to prevent things from slamming around in the back as we drive over treacherous terrain.

Depending on how many people live in your van, you may want more or less in your kitchen set up. If you have a gorgeous skoolie, you might not need a tote at all as you'll have significantly more room for cabinets, drawers, and other storage spaces. I simply provide this information as a guide to how little you can truly get away with packing while still being able to create delicious, healthy meals.

Cooking for Your Crowd

In the References section, I've included several links to recipe sources to help you get an idea of the types of meals you can make with just one burner, one pot, and one pan. Sure, it requires a little creativity, but you'll eventually get the hang of it. My cooking style when we first hit the road was "slop everything in a pot and make it taste good." This meant a lot of stews, stir frys, chilis, fajitas, and pasta with all of the veggies we needed to use up quickly thrown in. Honestly, it wasn't a bad strategy, given the "two meal" rule I mentioned earlier for fresh produce. That being said, there came a time when I felt like we were just eating slop after slop.

One of the most enjoyable parts of traveling the country is experiencing the local cuisine, as I mentioned earlier. But you don't have to do that exclusively at a restaurant. In Louisiana, for example, we stopped by a local market and picked up some amazing alligator sausages, which we grilled at a campsite and served over rice and veggies made with a local dry spice blend. We finished up the meal with a two-person pecan pie that we picked up at a bakery just a mile away from the campsite entrance. In Seattle, we feasted on a meal plucked directly from Pike Place Market, including cheese from Beecher's, salmon from Totem's Smokehouse, along with cherries and an avocado we picked up as we were strolling through the colorful stalls and aisles of the busy market. No cooking was required, and I'll always fondly remember that meal. We found an out-of-season camping spot by a lake several dozen miles away, and after a quick swim, we ate our feast out of the paper bags they came in while we watched the sunset, tired and dripping wet.

That being said, it's a little easier to cook for two unwavering foodies. If your diet, palette, or family include special requirements, you're obviously going to need to keep those at the forefront of your meal planning.

If anyone in your caravan has allergies, I strongly recommend eliminating ingredients that would cause an allergic reaction, simply because cross-contamination in tight quarters is extremely likely. This is, of course, ultimately up to you and your traveling companions, but my experiences with trying to keep a van clean (which we'll get to shortly, as well) have me erring on the side of caution.

If you are a parent who finds themselves cooking multiple meals for multiple picky children (or even grown family members) at home, you might want to find a way to streamline this experience on the road. For example, on stir fry night, let everyone choose their own veggies from the existing supply, and cook each plate individually. No substitutions, no replacements. Run your outdoor kitchen like a fast-paced diner! If someone doesn't want to participate in campfire chili, let them choose from one of the rainy day canned options, or perhaps enjoy a campfire quesadilla. While bread, buns, and rolls succumb easily to the elements, tortillas, naan, and pita tend to hold up well when the weather changes rapidly. Plus, if you're intrepid enough, you can make your own tortillas or naan with your cast iron skillet! Allowing for some variation on the menu isn't a problem, but cooking several different meals with one pot or pan and one burner will become time-consuming and frustrating very quickly. I know many van parents who have ended up having instant oatmeal and protein bars for dinner now and again just to create a compromise before bedtime!

A Drop About Hydration
One thing that is often forgotten in the context of van life is staying hydrated. When we're thirsty at home or in an office, we walk to the sink, water fountain, or water filter to pour a glass of water, drink it, and move on with our lives. In a van scenario, you may not have running water, or you may only have grey water. You'll also want to pay attention to the side effects of constant hydration, as well. You may not have a toilet in your van, which means you'll need to find public restroom stops as you travel or make like the bears and use the woods. I have to agree, all of this is a hassle.

At the same time, the side effects of dehydration aren't that pleasant, either. Headaches, muscle cramps, dizziness, and fatigue will put a real damper on your van adventure. You do need to drink plenty of water to keep your organs functioning and your mind alert.

One easy way to do this is to fill up on clean water every chance you get. Nearly every National Park has a free water station, where you can fill up your personal water bottles, or even reuse gallon jugs with fresh water for the next leg of your journey. If you're lucky enough to visit Hot Springs, there are spring water filling stations as well so you can take the famed healing waters on the road with you.

Reusable water bottles are ideal, but they do require cleaning and occasionally become damaged or leak. Don't take that as an opportunity to ignore hydration! Keep up with the cleanliness, and use disposable bottles as necessary to keep you healthy in the meantime. You can always drop them off at a recycling center later.

As you're enjoying the new flavors and snacks found around the country, look at beverage options as well. There are lots of interesting regional juices and sodas that deserve exploration. It's true that high amounts of sugar and caffeine aren't exactly great for your body, but as always, moderation is key.

The same can be said of alcohol, with an added note that you should never operate a van or skoolie under the influence. Brad and I are craft beer fans who visited many breweries on the first leg of our journey, and nearly every bartender checked in to make sure we were good before we tried to leave. It is much better to hang out in a parking lot for a few extra hours than to drive while buzzed. Instead, consider getting cans, bottles, or growlers to go, putting them in your cooler, and enjoying them after you've parked.

The last words of wisdom I'll offer when it comes to hydration are to always overstock on liquids. Weather can change quickly, and a rainy day can become a scorcher in what feels like an instant. There have been several times when Brad and I have thought we didn't need to pack water for a day of activities because the morning was cool, or the hike was short, or it was just a few miles to the next town. We deeply regretted that decision each and every time. Dehydration can be extremely dangerous, and affect you quickly, especially when you're outside, so err on the side of caution!

The temptation to snack more, to eat at restaurants more frequently, and to abandon everything we've learned about nutrition is very high when on the road. Without access to a full kitchen with adequate refrigeration, a large freezer, running water, and all the gadgets and gizmos that make meal prep so simple, you may feel a bit lost and overwhelmed. Take the time to browse recipes for new ideas. Spend some time at local markets to give each meal a unique flare. Consider multiple uses for each ingredient you buy. Most of all, be very mindful of food storage to ensure you aren't inviting bugs, critters, mold, or other contaminants into the van!

Chapter 3: Exercise: "Moving More Than a Van"

If one were to create a Venn diagram of people who love being outdoors and those who love van life, the overlap would be significant, if not a near-complete eclipse. It makes sense, of course. If you don't care for tall trees, a nice breeze, and the steady drone of mosquitos, you probably ought to choose a less untamed type of home.

In fact, many of the people who have chosen van life do so because of the proximity to nature and the ability to experience so much of the beauty and wilderness that is still abundant on this planet. That means ample opportunities to hike, climb, canoe, bike, and participate in all of the amazing outdoor sports and activities that bring us closer to peace and harmony with Earth itself.

All of this outdoor adventuring requires a lot of energy, and many van nomads log hundreds – if not thousands – of miles outside of the van. But there's one fact that is often overlooked; you have to drive hundreds – if not thousands - of miles to get from place to place. The unfortunate truth is that some days will be dedicated to sunrise to sunset driving, with no hiking, no biking, and little activity besides getting out of the van, filling up with gas, and getting back into the van.

Additionally, not every day is going to be perfect for outdoor activities. Rock climbing in a lightning storm is a pretty bad idea. Canoeing on ice requires specialized equipment. There are days when even taking a little walk around your campsite may seem like a major and unnecessary undertaking, either because of your physical status, your mental or emotional state, or just plain gross weather. If you're working from the road, you may find it oc-casionally difficult to fit in those all-day hikes when you have meetings or looming deadlines as well.

All of these factors compound the importance of maintaining physical fitness while living in a van. The good news is that there are several things you can do to keep yourself feeling great and ready to take on spontaneous adventures, even when the weather, your travel plans, or your mind and body don't want to cooperate.

A few things before we get started:

1.	Don't do any type of exercise that doesn't feel good. Everyone has some kind of limitation, so don't push yourself beyond what you can comfortably do today. Just because you saw someone else do it on social media, because you feel like you ought to be able to do it, or because I mentioned it here in this book, doesn't mean you should rush out to bend yourself into a specific routine.

	In my case, I spent my teenage years and early twenties working with rescue horses. As a result, I have a lot of unpredictable limitations in my body. Combine that with the fact that I am clumsy enough to break and sprain things just walking across a room, and you're probably wincing as hard as all of the physical therapists I've worked with over the years. I creak. I don't bend correctly. And that's totally okay, because that's just how my body is.

So, the number one rule is to work with your body. Don't force it. Push yourself, but not into the danger zone. Listen to your joints and muscles. Listen to your medical support team. Most importantly, if climbing mountains makes you want to punch a tree (guilty) don't do it!

2. Don't feel like you need to do anything just because #vanlife stars on social media do it. The first major disappointment I had about living in a van was that it is not pretty. There are tons of pictures online of gorgeous, perfectly toned young men and women with perfect skin and hair, in their gleaming white vans, wearing stylish bathing suits, romping around with their equally beautiful children, or staring peacefully at the sun setting over a picturesque beach.

    When I look back at the pictures from our first year living in a van, I feel like I can smell Brad and myself through the photographs. There will be dirt, mud, sand, and bugs. There will be stink. In fact, there will be all kinds of stink from all sorts of sources while you figure out your own process. You will have to go to the bathroom in the wilderness at some point, and you may not be graceful. You will probably run out of water at some point and have to deal with sticky, sand-filled hair. You will sweat from places you didn't know could produce sweat.

    So, let's go ahead and abandon that perfect social media picture, okay? Swerving back into reality, not every van lifer hikes, bikes, or climbs. I've heard whispers that you're not really a van person until you've done Angel's Landing, or you're not a hiker if you haven't done the Grand Canyon. That's all bunk. If you want to do Angel's Landing, go for it. Be safe. Send me pictures. Everyone experiences the planet in different ways that are meaningful and enjoyable for them. Don't make yourself miserable because you think you need to do something, and don't be hard on yourself if these goals are not accessible to you.

Here's my true-life example: Brad and I did the Mighty Five in Utah in May of 2018. To the uninitiated, that's Arches, Canyonlands, Capitol Reef, Bryce Canyon, and Zion national parks, back-to-back. We started with Canyonlands, and my inner mountain goat was having a blast, hopping from rock to rock, following mysteriously placed cairns across the tops of wind-swept plateaus. And then, because I'm me, I misjudged a foot-wide hop from one rocky outcrop to another, and slid in between the rocks, twisting my ankle on the way. At the time, it was no big deal – I walked it out, finished the hike, and loved every minute of it.

The next day at Capitol Reef, I found the going pretty tough. At Arches, I was pretty much dragging my swollen foot. Then, I made the critical error of green-lighting the Navajo-Peekaboo Trail at Bryce Canyon, which is approximately five miles in length with nearly 1,500-foot elevation gain, and I fell apart. By the time we got to Zion, I couldn't tell you which hurt more, my ankle or my pride.

So, the moral of the story is that there is no such thing as the perfect social media-washed #vanlifer. Pushing past that point of comfort, fitness, and desire will only end in tears and the need for medical treatment.

With that advice in hand, let's take a look at some of the types of exercise that are conducive to van living. We'll focus on how to stay in shape while you're actively on the road and helpful tips for finding fitness outlets when you feel like mixing it up a bit.

Regular Activity for Those Who Wander

Hiking, biking, climbing, and paddling aren't the only activities available to those who live in a van. It is perfectly okay to go for the occasional walk to wander around, get fresh air, and explore the scenery. While hiking often includes long trails, varied landscape, and obstacles of different levels of difficulty, you can pause for a minute to take a slow, easy, and pointless walk. Look at the different types of trees. Focus on your surroundings more than logging the miles.

If speed is more your thing, go for a jog! There are plenty of trails around the country that are absolutely beautiful and manicured for joggers and runners to take advantage of. Many national parks offer horseback riding trails, which are a great workout for the core and legs, and an amazing way to experience the gorgeous settings. Go for a swim, or rent an inner tube and do a float/hike combination down a nearby waterway. Don't feel you have to do the same thing over and over!

There are plenty of exercises that translate well to the outdoor experience which might surprise you. Doing Yin Yoga on the beach in Hawaii opened up my eyes to the fact that I didn't need a studio with a guru giving me directions in order to enjoy my practice. In fact, I found that breaking up a long hike with a few intervals of yoga poses, such as a quick Sun Salutation, or a Warrior/Sun flow, helped me avoid stiffness in my lower back and hamstrings. If you're not interested in doing chaturangas in the dirt, don't worry about bringing your mat, a softer spot with no rocks or branches, and a towel should do the trick!

Speaking of intervals, you can also incorporate high intensity interval training (HIIT) moves into your van life as well. HIIT workouts may seem impossible outside of the gym, but Tabata circuits of burpees, squats, lunges, mountain climbers, and planks are all bodyweight exercises that can be done absolutely anywhere. As an added bonus, no one will be around to hear you curse while you do burpees.

"Extended Driving Pose" Is Not An Exercise
What about those days during which you spend more time seated behind the wheel than you do standing or moving? If you've ever driven twelve hours straight, you are aware of the physical and mental strain it can put

on a person. First, your behind goes completely numb. Then, your legs start to hurt and your shoulders get tense from holding onto the wheel. If you drive an elderly vehicle with a sense of humor, your fingers probably get a little numb and tingly from trying to accommodate for the lack of power steering. Your lumbar region starts to feel like a jigsaw puzzle put together incorrectly. Your head hurts, none of your music is worth listening to, and you start to dream of a heating pad, a massage, and one of those astronaut beds they advertise on late night infomercials.

If you've never driven twelve hours straight, don't let this description dissuade you from trying. The key to keeping the body happy during long hauls is movement. While there are very few exercises you can actually do behind the wheel, this is a good time to take advantage of the notoriously low fuel economy of your van or skoolie, and move every time you stop for gas.

When I say "move," I mean really move. Not the casual "nobody's watching, right?" micro stretches you can do while pumping your gas or scraping insect carcasses off of your vehicle's front end. I mean, really go for it and get the blood flowing again.

There are several ways you can do this. My recommendation would be to incorporate at least one exercise from each section of this chart before you hop back into the van again. If you're bold, do them right there in the parking lot. If you're less enthusiastic about making a scene in your travel clothes with car seat hair, try sneaking into the back of your vehicle or the restroom - the walk will do you good!

Basic Stretches	**Road Yoga**	**Cardio**
• Bend over and touch your toes	• Mountain pose to forward fold, halfway lift, back to mountain pose	• Walk rapidly in place while you pump your gas (yes, people will look at you strangely, but your legs and spine will LOVE it)
• Reach all the way to the sky	• Warrior 1 and Reverse Warrior (Peaceful Warrior)	• Jumping jacks
• Stand on your tippy-toes, then relax through your heels (best done on a curb so you can stretch all the way through!)	• Side Angle/ Extended Side Angle Pose (or variations)	• High knees
	• Chair pose	• Goblet squats (substitute a water bottle for a kettlebell)
• Reach your arm down the side of your leg to the ground	• Low lunge to Runner's Lunge	• Jog around the parking lot for a few minutes
• Slow long lunges	• Supine Twists (you may want to do these in the back of your van)	• Use a curb or sidewalk for a few minutes of step ups
• Stand with legs hip-width apart and touch the opposite hand to opposite toes	• Downward Facing Dog (again, you probably don't want to put your hands on the parking lot or bathroom floor)	• Squat jumps
• Chest openers	• Extended triangle pose	• Incline push ups against the van
• Small circles and big circles in both directions (do this with your head, your arms, your hands, and your ankles for a full-body release!)		

These are just a few examples, of course. Your body will tell you exactly what type of motion is going to feel best when you get out of the driver's seat. Speaking of which, I'd like to caution you to always exit your van slowly, and pay attention to where your feet might be landing. I can't tell you how many times Brad and I have managed to fall out of the driver's seat because we underestimated how rubbery and unsteady our legs were after a long stretch of driving. Additionally, take your time when fully standing up. Orthostatic hypotension (drops in your blood pressure) is a very real thing, and if you think doing jumping jacks at a gas pump is too embarrassing, you'll definitely not want to faint at one! Take your time swinging in and out of your vehicle to avoid any injury or awkwardness.

Outside of the Outdoors

There may also be times when you crave indoor fitness. If you're a very outdoorsy person, this may not make sense right off the bat, but there are many reasons why you might find yourself longing for the gym or a workout class.

The first is air conditioning. A controlled, indoor environment is going to provide a lot of advantages for those who are trying to "level up" with their outdoor activities. There are many scales available that rate various hikes, climbs, and summits as different grades or classes, based on how difficult they are to complete. As you "climb" the ranks (pun mostly intended), you'll need to gain certain physical attributes and abilities in order to be successful. If your van or skoolie is not the right environment for building those upper body muscles, or gaining strength in your legs, you may wish to check out a gym or fitness group to boost your workouts.

You may also just want a change of pace. I discovered in my early 20s that a boxing class here and there is wonderful for relieving my anxiety and frustration. Since there are few things in nature that tolerate jabs, punches, and kicks quite like a punching bag, the most ideal outlet for this type of release is a dedicated boxing gym.

Lastly, you might just want the company. We'll talk about all of the interesting things van life can do to your mental health in a bit, but many of us are hardwired to really enjoy exercising in groups. Whether that means taking an aerobics class or Aqua Zumba or swinging from a TRX strap, you may find a great deal of enjoyment in working out with others. There's camaraderie and a touch of competition. Best of all, you're not suffering alone.

When these urges appear, go ahead and indulge them, if you're financially capable of doing so at that moment. Many gyms or studios have a "drop in" policy that you can easily find on their website or by giving them a quick call. For a reduced rate, you can usually appear once, take advantage of the equipment or teacher's knowledge, enjoy your workout, enjoy the showers with endless hot water, and be on your way. Always check it out ahead of time, though, so you know when to arrive, and abide by any dress codes or other policies. Some studios or gyms require specific footwear, for example, or ask that drop-ins only come during specific non-peak hours. Usually these notes are posted on the website, so you aren't taken by surprise.

Another option is to find a gym or club with national access. This is a relatively new phenomenon, but there are many chain gyms that allow members to use any of their locations across the United States. Again, I recommend double-checking policies ahead of time to be adequately prepared, but there is something very convenient about being able to stop by a completely new-to-you gym in a state you've never visited before and knocking out a few miles on the treadmill before hopping back in your van and heading out again. And yes, included-with-membership showers and massage chairs are a fantastic added bonus.

You can also take advantage of municipal Health Trails. The actual name used will depend on your location, of course, but the concept is the same. Along a few miles of walking, biking, or hiking trails, there will be a variety of obstacles or fitness challenges set up. The instructions are posted so you know how to properly execute the exercise, along with a recommend-ed number of reps or time allotted to complete the practice. Often, the equipment can be multi-purposed for several different exercises, such as balance beams that can be used for step ups, or a bar that can be used for pull-ups or knee raises.

Locating these types of trails may seem like a daunting challenge, since they go by many different names, but I suggest starting with a search for "trails near me," and refining from there. Terms like "fitness," "wellness," and "challenge" are frequent indicators that a trail features some additional obstacles to help you add variety to your overall workout routine.

Again, it's important to note that you should not feel obligated to do anything that is uncomfortable, unrealistic, or potentially dangerous. Always stretch before and after you exercise. When going on long adventures, be sure to pack plenty of water and snacks to fuel your body, particularly snacks that are high in protein and energy. Be mindful of your body's warning signs, and if you feel discomfort approaching, find a way to safely end the activity and return to the van as quickly as possible.

This section may seem like a bunch of obvious reminders. Go to the doctor. Brush your teeth. Eat your vegetables. Get some exercise. At the heart of it, yes, those are all things many of us learned in elementary school, if not before. Nevertheless, there's something magical that happens any time we make huge changes in our lives that often causes us to abandon some of the things we know we ought to do as we adapt to our new method of survival.

If you find yourself six months into your van quest, and you haven't yet seen a dentist, do not despair. This doesn't mean you're an unhealthy or neglectful person. You've obviously had much bigger things on your mind, like where to go next, finding a place to sleep and rest every night, how to deal with road problems, possible van breakdowns, and more. Forgive yourself and make it up to yourself in the near future.

The same goes for eating healthfully and getting enough exercise. If you find that you're not where you want to be, give yourself some grace, set new goals, and act more conscientiously. I know that's easier said than done, especially if you have mile after mile of endless driving to rehash all of your mistakes.

But let's be honest – adapting to van life is hard. It's like moving into a new apartment every single day for the first several months. You have no idea where anything is. You're not sure if the furniture is in the right place. It is possible to run out of water, and sometimes you don't have enough power to charge your phone. Unusual problems will arise. You're trying to build routines when very little is the same from day to day. You're allowed to have a few hiccups in practical living.

Hopefully, the reminders in this book will help you either stay on the path of preventive care, or at least make it easier to navigate back to a regular wellness outlook if you find yourself straying. If you haven't started your voyage yet, I hope that you're able to use these points and reminders as a jumping-off place for integrating the basic preventive care you practice at home into your less domesticated van lifestyle. At the very least, you'll have a new collection of tricks, tips, and van life hacks that you can incorporate into your next adventure!

Section 3: Managing Less Than Perfect Health on the Road

I'd love to tell you that if you do everything exactly right from the last section, that you'll always be healthy and happy. Unfortunately, the human body doesn't work like that. You can see every doctor you need on a regular basis, wash your hands copiously, eat the largest quantities of the freshest vegetables possible, hydrate to perfection, and still fall prey to illness or injury.

When we get sick or injured while living in a house, condo, or apartment, the solution is obvious; we climb into bed or make a nest on the sofa, and rest in between watching daytime television, nibbling on crackers, sipping ginger ale, and downing our preferred medications. We have ice packs and heating pads and plenty of pillows to pad our sick beds, and it's generally just a short, wobbly trip to the bathroom.

On the road, all of that is turned on its head. Of course, you can turn your sleeping area into a nest for recuperation, and if your van or skoolie has a bathroom, it's going to be closer than ever. But there are also many less convenient aspects to being sick or injured in a van. You have to decide whether to push on, or stay put. You need to find places to rest more frequently. You have to be more concerned about spreading germs. If you're injured, even getting in and out of the van can become tricky.

My number one recommendation is to be as prepared as possible for illnesses and injuries. In this section, we'll take a look at dealing with both chronic conditions and emergency situations in the context of van life. During our first year on the road, I think Brad and I managed to experience the worst bout of health-related situations we'd had in years, so a lot of the information I'll present is based on my own anecdotes. However, everyone on the road has issues at some point. So, I've pulled in a lot of thoughts and recommendations from experts in healthcare and van-life, and sometimes both. These tips help guide us all through what are often the worst days of our van journey.

Disclaimer: This Book Is Not a Doctor

One quick disclaimer before we proceed: Always follow your physician's advice when it comes to your medical care. The following tips are not intended to replace any recommendations from healthcare professionals. While you are ultimately in charge of your own wellness, please consider the guidelines shared with you by actual, trained medical staff over anything I suggest. I don't know the ins and outs of your life, your health status, or your abilities. I'm just a van lifer who learned things the hard way sharing what I learned with other van lifers, so they don't have to learn it the hard way!

Chapter 1: Managing Chronic Conditions from Anywhere and Everywhere

We touched a bit on dealing with maintenance medication and chronic conditions in the previous section, but I wanted to dive a little deeper into what it means to live on the road with a condition that won't just simply clear up on its own one day.

There's a lot of undue stigma about those who suffer from chronic conditions. The prevalent opinion is that, if people take good care of themselves through preventive care, they will not experience chronic conditions later in life. While there's some validity to that claim, many chronic conditions are based less on lifestyle choices and more on genetics, environmental factors, or sheer chance.

The term "chronic condition" refers to any health condition that persists for longer than three months and includes:
- Alcohol Use Disorder
- Alzheimer's Disease and Related Dementia Arthritis (Osteoarthritis and Rheumatoid)
- Asthma
- Atrial Fibrillation
- Autism Spectrum Disorders
- Cancer (Breast, Colorectal, Lung, Prostate, etc.)
- Chronic Kidney Disease
- Chronic Obstructive Pulmonary Disease (COPD)

- Crohn's Disease
- Cystic Fibrosis
- Depression
- Diabetes
- Epilepsy
- Heart Failure
- Hepatitis B & C
- HIV/AIDS
- Hyperlipidemia (High cholesterol)
- Hypertension (High blood pressure)
- Ischemic Heart Disease
- Multiple Sclerosis
- Osteoporosis
- Parkinson's Disease
- Schizophrenia and Other Mental Illnesses
- Stroke
- Substance Use Disorders

I have both good news and bad news. Bad news first: Generally speaking, living in a van will not make your chronic condition go away. Here's the good news, though. Living in a van is still very much a possibility for many people coping with chronic conditions. There are certain lifestyle changes associated with van living, such as reduced stress, less air pollution, and increased physical activity, that can have a positive impact on some of the symptoms of certain chronic conditions.

That doesn't mean it will be a walk in the park. I was diagnosed with a chronic condition in 2008. So far, things have been well maintained with medication, regular check-ins with my medical support team, and even therapy as needed to help me through the rough spots. There are good days and bad days. I have been hospitalized due to complications from my condition, and I learned how to be more aware of what causes difficulties and what warning signs to look for.

Therefore, I will always recommend that anyone living with chronic conditions make their well-being a priority to prevent larger complications in the long-run.

Be Open With Your Care Team
The first thing I encourage anyone with a persistent medical situation to do is speak to their medical care team about their plans to live on the road.

When I first broached the subject with my primary care provider, I was expecting her to tell me she had never heard such a horrible idea. She did not. In fact, she told me she was jealous, started telling me about all sorts of cool places I needed to check out, and gave me a few pointers for starting my blog. Then, we got into the 'Real Talk' portion of the appointment where we discussed how to get my medications, how to store them properly, and what to do if I miss a dose on the road. We then scheduled our next follow-up appointment as a video conference, along with a few resources I could tap into if things started to slide sideways while I was on the road.

Most importantly, she reminded me of something I hadn't considered: It's okay to take care of yourself. By this, she meant that if I have to put a pause on van life, circle back home more frequently, or in any manner stop adventuring because I needed to prioritize myself, it's not some huge failure. It's hitting the proverbial pause button before you're forced to hit full stop and eject.

I've mentioned the #vanlife ego a few times, and I'll mention it again. There seems to be this odd social pressure to drop out of society and succeed, but if you need to make van life a part-time thing, a small radius thing, or take a break and check into a hotel for a while, it does not make you any less of a van lifer. It doesn't mean you've failed in any shape or form.

If you are currently receiving treatment for a chronic illness, by all means, you can still explore the world, as long as you have the green light from your medical team. Perhaps that means you don't sell your home and go off the grid right away, but instead, you explore a smaller radius around your home base while treatment is ongoing. Maybe that means being a "weekend warrior" for a period of time.

Once you've got the official "go ahead" from your medical team, determine if virtual check-ins are a good idea for you and where you are in treatment. Since the COVID-19 pandemic, many physicians have adapted to video conferencing for check-ins or non-emergency appointments in which labs (such as bloodwork, urinalysis, or other samples) are not required. If this is an option for you, be sure to position your van so that at the time of your appointments, you are in a secure, quiet, well-lit area with a strong WiFi signal. Make sure that the phone or laptop you'll be using has enough charge to make it through the appointment. Another kind reminder is to make sure you're taking the time zones into account. Since van lifers are notorious for losing track of what day it is, be sure to set a reminder on your phone so you don't miss your check-in entirely.

Medication Tips

Medications can be tricky on the road, as mentioned earlier. While using national chain pharmacies can help with obtaining your prescriptions, there are many types of prescriptions that require frequent updates from your physician to measure its effectiveness and any potentially harmful side effects. Make sure you talk to your team about your van plans so that you can adequately schedule both your appointments and travel. Missing an appointment – and thus a refill – can be incredibly harmful to your continued well-being, so make sure you stay on top of your schedule. Additionally, if you're going to miss an appointment due to unforeseen events, such as a van breakdown, bad weather, or other delays, talk to your provider as soon as possible. You don't want to wait longer than you need to for that appointment and subsequent refill.

Storing prescriptions can also be difficult. If you have prescriptions that are temperature sensitive, I recommend not taking your chances with low-tech options like a cooler. There are several tiny refrigerators on the market that can plug into your dash and won't drain your battery. By "tiny," I mean, they can fit a few cans of soda. These are often the perfect size for medications, as they can be stashed in the front of the van without the chance of tumbling around in the back. Check out your local supermarket or department store to see what options they have.

This may seem like a strange dictive, but I also recommend storing your medication in a way that you'll be able to remember whether or not you've taken them. For example, those day-of-the-week pill organizers can be incredibly helpful. When you're on the road, days tend to blur into each other and your medication routine may feel a bit disrupted.

Years ago, I trained our dog to beg for a treat every time I needed to take my medications, and as a result, I could never forget. Our old beagle would start notifying me that 'Treat Time' was coming up about fifteen minutes before I needed to take my pills. Pretty soon, I had trained my own internal clock to start anticipating this daily interruption.

On the road, however, time starts to lose meaning. You wake up when you wake up, and you go to bed when you go to bed. Aside from any potential client meetings or deadlines, days and hours seem meaningless. Your internal clock has basically given up, and there's little sense of routine. I've actually got a little two-sided sign that I flip to remind myself of medication status. One side says, "You're Good." The other says "Take Your Meds, Dear." I flip the sign to "You're Good" after I take my meds each morning, and flip it to "Take Your Meds, Dear" before I go to bed for the night. Is there plenty of room for human error? Absolutely! Yet so far, I've been pretty good about keeping track of where I am on my schedule, and hopefully you'll be inspired to create a system of alarms, alerts, or signs that work for you.

In a nutshell, managing a chronic condition from the road is entirely possible. You may have to make adjustments to your travel schedule or include certain accommodations to your overall plan, but unless your medical team specifically forbids it, there's a version of van life that is accessible to nearly everyone. Whether you have to temporarily scale back, or make very deliberate and thoughtful plans for your daily endeavors, you can find a way to incorporate van life into your lifestyle.

Chapter 2: When Bad Things Happen

Regardless of your best efforts, you will find yourself under the weather at some point. It is my greatest hope that your van life be blessed with the best health at all times. However, the truth is that we all come down with a bug here or there, or find an exciting way to accidentally damage ourselves through the course of daily activities. Perhaps that's just my own clumsy experience, but in any lifestyle with increased activity, the chances of experiencing minor sprains and strains greatly multiply.

Preparing for Minor Disasters

As I mentioned in the beginning of this chapter, being prepared is key. The literal last thing you want to do when you're ill or injured is drag yourself to the pharmacy and fill your cart with a bunch of things that may or may not make you feel better. That's unnecessary exposure to the outside world, and you'll probably end up impulse buying supplies you don't really need, simply because you're desperate to feel better.

Instead, create a Medical Preparation Kit before you kick off your van life. Since real estate is at a premium inside the van, the contents of this kit should focus on things that are likely to happen to you and your family, along with some vital "just in case" type elements. In my opinion, the Med Prep Kit is more important than extra undergarments if that helps emphasize how crucial it is to really plan this part out!

You'll definitely want to include at least a basic first aid kit in your MPK. I don't just mean a multi-pack of adhesive bandages and a tube of antiseptic ointment, either. I mean an **actual first aid kit** that includes things like:

- Gauze dressing pads of various sizes (at least large and small sizes)
- Trauma pads

- Gauze roll bandages
- First aid tape roll
- Instant cold compress
- A basic triangular sling
- Adhesive bandages in every size imaginable, including Elbow/Knee patch size (2"x4"), junior size (⊠" x 1 ½ "), fingertip and knuckle type, and 1" and ¾" sizes
- Thermometer
- Triple antibiotic ointment
- Antiseptic cleaning wipes
- Hydrocortisone cream
- Aloe/Multipurpose burn cream
- Tweezers
- Scissors
- Coban-style self-adhesive wrap
- Extra clean towels
- Paper towels
- Box of disposable facial tissues (at least one)
- Duct tape

These types of first aid kits can be found at many retailers already packaged in an easy-store waterproof container and usually have a handy first aid guidebook tucked inside. Of course, you can easily build your own using this as a shopping list. I would definitely recommend making sure you have a waterproof, airtight bag or box to store these items in, and definitely spring for the guidebook as well. You may think that first aid is pretty intuitive - or at least easily Googled - until you find yourself deep in the Ozarks with no phone service, wondering how panicked you should get about a mysterious rash.

But don't stop there! There are a lot of situations that need more than bandages and a book! As my aunties recommended, having naproxen, acetaminophen, AND ibuprofen on hand isn't a bad idea. In addition, bear in mind that you don't have to purchase giant economy-sized bottles of each, unless you already go through that much at home. A small bottle will be enough to get you through the early stages of any minor ailment, and can be replenished as necessary.

If you're an allergy sufferer (as many of us are), you may want to speak to your physician about your allergy situation and come up with a backup plan, especially if this is your first time travelling extensively out of state. Your body is about to encounter brand new pollen and spores and all sorts of allergy triggers that it may never have experienced before. Depending on your current triggers and allergic responses, you might need a backup medication or epinephrine injectable on hand to prevent an unforeseen emergency. A bottle of saline nasal flush may also be something you want to keep on hand to reduce allergic responses. If your allergies can trigger an asthma attack, make sure you have emergency inhalers at the ready in your Med Prep Kit as well.

Then there's what I call the "multipurpose solution." This includes items that can assist with a variety of conditions. For example, menthol cough drops can soothe an irritated throat or cough, provide relief to an upset stomach (but can irritate heartburn symptoms, so be careful there), and even quell anxiety by encouraging deep, meaningful breathing. A menthol chest rub can also feel very nice on sore muscles and feet. A bottle of non-talc powder with calamine can be extremely helpful when dealing with chafing, burning, rashes, insect bites and stings, and help you feel less gross when it's been a long stretch between bathing opportunities.

I also recommend having a few over-the-counter remedies on hand in case something pops up. This includes a bismuth subsalicylate, like Pepto-Bismol, or similar product that can stave off upset stomachs and diarrhea. Both a daytime multi-symptom formula, and a nighttime multi-symptom formula for cold and flu are a good investment. Head colds are common anytime and anywhere, and being in a moving vehicle while you're feeling stuffy and snotty is just very uncomfortable.

Brad and I picked up some kind of bug just before we hit Virginia. I was going through a box of tissues a day by myself, and I could tell that Brad was just miserable. I had long been looking forward to doing an overnight hike at Shenandoah National Park, but what really happened is that Brad parked the van at a beautiful overlook so we could take a nap in the back. We ended up having to stop every few hours for a rest period. We pulled the daytime liquid from the Med Prep Kit and made a lot of hot tea with honey on our propane burner to help our aching heads, throats, and sinuses.

In the first year of van life, I would say we used everything in our Med Prep Kit except the adhesive bandages. I ended up using a lot of Coban and gauze wrap for my assorted sprains and strains. We both went through our fair share of cough drops, especially when I ended up getting tonsillitis in New England. The Pepto Bismol came in handy after a particularly violent encounter with some dubious chicken wings in Oregon too.

When preparing your own Med Prep Kit, think about what you use regularly at home. You'll also want to consider the types of malaise you and your family find most bothersome and frequent. While a first aid kit is a good start, build the rest of your kit around your own reality. This chart provides some helpful examples:

If You Experience...	Then Consider Packing...
Discomfort/Allergic Reactions to Bug Bites and Stings	- Instant ice packs - Insect repellent - Calamine lotion or hydrocortisone cream - Antihistamines - Oatmeal-based soap - Epinephrine injectable for severe allergic reaction
Frequent sprains and strains	- Support braces for weak joints or painful areas - Self-adhesive wraps - Cream/lotion/ointment for sore muscles - Battery operated TENS unit or other massage device, such as myofascial massage balls or foam roller - Instant ice packs - Extra towels or wash clothes for cold compresses - Maximum strength pain reliever
Migraine Headaches	- Instant caffeine source - Migraine relief medication (eg, Excedrin Migraine) - Sleep mask to keep the light out - Instant ice packs - Ear plugs
Frequent Head Colds	- Daytime cold medication - Nighttime cold medication - Vitamin supplements - Tea bags and honey (if you have a propane burner or other method for heating water quickly) - Throat lozenges- heavy duty and regular strength

As you read through this chart, you'll probably have moments of "Oh, I didn't think about that." and "That definitely doesn't apply to me." Those thoughts should be the basis for completing a chart like this that does resonate with the daily health needs of you and your family. Prepare for the unknown, but REALLY PREPARE for the known.

Amazingly, I didn't consider my frequent bouts of tonsillitis in the early months of Autumn until I was in complete agony somewhere in Vermont.

Instead of being prepared, I did exactly what I just told you not to do; I made Brad pull over at the first drug store we found, and I bought three different types of lozenges, two enormous bottles of NyQuil, a multipack of Puffs Plus infused with Vicks, dissolvable zinc tablets, a giant bottle of Vitamin C capsules, a box of Theraflu, and a little stuffed fish toy because I was feeling dumpy and it made me smile. I spent far more money than I needed to spend and bought a whole bunch of stuff I ended up using for a week at most. That meant we had to keep hauling it, which became redundant, and all it did after I started feeling better was take up space and get in the way.

Instead, I should have packed the one type of lozenge I use at home, quality tissues, zinc tablets, and NyQuil before we even left. The moment I started feeling a scratchy throat come on, I should've upped the Vitamin C. I don't regret the stuffed fish at all though. We named him Mr. Ferguson, and he's one of the van's mascots.

As far as storing your Med Prep Kit, I recommend giving it its own tote. That way, you'll know exactly where things are at all times, or at least where they should be. Make sure that this tote is always easily accessible too. As always, I recommend airtight and watertight totes to prevent infestation, mold, and dirt, since you want this kit to be in pristine condition at all times. Also, be sure to check the expiration dates on the creams and medications from time to time. They're not as effective if they're expired, and since time has no meaning on the road, you don't want to find this out in an emergency!

Before you even roll your van out on your first excursion, make sure you're prepared for the most common eventualities. While one of the main draws of van life is its unpredictable nature, there are certain health situations that you'll want to be able to head off quickly. Having a well-stocked, fully-intentional Med Prep Kit in your van is a great way to keep your everyday ouchies and yuckies at a minimum.

What to Do When Things Get Worse

While most situations and symptoms can be treated on the go, you might occasionally find yourself completely wiped out by illness or injury.

Let me make this first part abundantly clear: That's okay. If you need to rest, please rest.

There seems to be this van life ego or bravada that stopping and resting somehow detracts from your experience. Perhaps it's because I'm older, or maybe it has to do with how many different breaks I had to take due to illness and injury, but there is absolutely no shame in taking time to let your body heal from whatever malady is currently haunting you. There's not a soul on this planet who wants you to share your germs if you happen to be ill, so just don't.

What to do when you're more than a little sick or hurt is directly related to your van setup. If you can successfully quarantine yourself within your van for a week or so while you wait for the worst to pass, that's ideal. Just make sure you have plenty of liquids, a nearby bathroom, adequate bedding, excellent air flow, and plenty of mindless activities to occupy yourself between nap times.

When you read the recommendations for any type of healing, "rest" always tops the list. Don't let some preconceived notion of what you ought to do take you away from what you need to do to help your body. Sure, you can push forward, but will you really enjoy it? As I mentioned earlier, I had a bout of tonsillitis in New England. I actually continued hiking through the symptoms until I nearly passed out on a trail. But, I insisted that we keep driving for several days. There were a few times I accompanied Brad in the van to the trailhead, and while he got to wander blissfully through the Adirondacks, traipse through Baxter State Park, and meander meaningfully through White Mountain National Forest, I laid in the back of the van intermittently sleeping and taking cold medicine.

So, why did I say, "Let's keep going!" even though I was miserable? Because I thought that's what van lifers do. Nowhere on social media was there a guidebook for what to do when your tonsils are the size of your fist. If I had been at home, I would've gone to my regular family doctor, gotten some medication, and snuggled into bed with hot tea and *The Price Is Right*. I felt like because I was on the road, I had to keep being on the road.

During my bout with tonsillitis, the local temperatures reached the mid-30s Fahrenheit at night. I was simultaneously too hot and too cold, depending on the time of day. We had no onboard electricity, running water, or toilet, which put serious limitations on my ability to have constant fluids. While I tried to make it work, we ended up finding a delightful - yet spartan - cottage in which I could spend a few nights recuperating. Being indoors and having the ability to fully rest, along with the amazing soup from a local cafe and a whole bunch of orange juice, did quite a bit to bring me back to health.

That is why, as I write this book, I strongly recommend rest to anyone who needs it. Unless you are on a dire timeline, don't feel that you need to push yourself to the breaking point to fulfill the "Ultimate Van Lifestyle."

Additionally, there is no shame in visiting a local Urgent Care. Just because you live in a van doesn't mean you're immortal! Urgent Care can be a great, low-cost stop for most general issues from a cough that won't go away to hiking accidents.

Before you go, make sure the Urgent Care you visit has the services you need. This may sound obvious, but I have personally experienced a city with multiple Urgent Care centers that all provide different services. To avoid the hassle of being transferred to the pricey emergency room (ER) or driving around looking for another location, be sure that if you're injured, the location you're heading to has digital x-ray services. If you're ill, make sure they can prescribe medications. If you can check the waitlist times online, all the better.

Sometimes, however, you actually need the ER. If you are experiencing any of the following symptoms, don't bother with looking up the ideal Urgent Care; instead, go immediately to the ER:

- Shortness of breath/difficulty breathing or swallowing
- Obvious bone breaks
- Bleeding that will not stop
- Head injury with loss of consciousness
- Unexplainable chest/abdominal pains
- Animal bites or attacks
- Stroke symptoms
- Fevers over 100 degrees Fahrenheit
- Burns to the hand or face, or greater than 3 inches in size
- When symptoms are persistent and don't respond to treatment

If you are living with a chronic condition, heed your care team's advice on when to head to the ER. If it's after hours for Urgent Care, yet symptoms are making it impossible to comfortably dwell in your van for the night, it is also reasonable to head to the Emergency Room for immediate care.

Perfect health is not a guarantee, and without the comforts of home, finding yourself under the weather for the first time while living on the road can be a bit of a shock to the system. However, it's not impossible to manage everything from chronic health conditions to the occasional cold or injury.

The two main things to factor in are preparedness and the ability to rest when you need to. During times of flare ups, illness, or injury, you might need to be more deliberate in your every move, but don't take this as a sign that the gods of the road want you to go home.

Over time, you'll have all of your self-care patterns down to a science. You'll learn new routines to replace those that you learned in your stationary home. You'll gain a better perspective of what you need to keep yourself well on the road. You'll probably make a few mistakes, but you'll definitely learn from them. From figuring out the best way to dispose of your used tissues and medical supplies, to storing your meds in places that make sense for how and when you take them, you'll need to pay a little more attention at first, but eventually your routine will emerge.

And when things take a turn for the worse? Don't be afraid to seek additional assistance. Allow yourself to stop and get the rest you need. You deserve to feel better quickly, so give your body the best chance it can to recuperate completely.

Section 4: A Brief Section about Housekeeping and Hygiene

You might think housekeeping is a little out of place for a book that claims to address "health and wellness issues." This section will be shorter than the others because it would be impossible for me to tell you how to clean your personal living space with so many different cleaning methods, products, and needs based on your own system and the design of your van, skoolie, or RV.

Therefore, this is going to be a high-level overview about basic hygienic needs in a van. I have no doubt that each and every reader of this book is familiar with the need to clean all surfaces, change bed linens, do laundry, and bathe once in a while. These are skills that we're all proficient at to some degree or another.

When you take your life on the road, however, things change. There is no "pants chair." There is limited space for your intricate sorting method for clothing at various stages of the clean-to-dirty spectrum. If your floor is dirty, your feet will be dirty, and thus your bed will be dirty, and so on. There is limited room to avoid filth, so your ability to ignore a little momentary grossness is often compromised.

Imagine, if you will, a container of leftover soup. Perhaps you take this leftover soup out of the cooler in an attempt to reach a water bottle below it. Maybe you forget that the soup is sitting next to the cooler and go to bed. The consequence for this minor mishap, as Brad and I can attest, is your van smelling like soup for 3-4 days. This is compounded by a devout following of insects, despite driving with all possible windows open and creating a wind vortex in the back.

Cleanliness matters in a van. Whether you just want to be able to sleep without wondering what that stink is, or you're intent on managing allergies and preventing growth of any nasty bacteria around the van, keep in mind that just a little bit of cleaning can go a long way. Let's take a quick look at some of the simple things you can do to keep a tidy home on the road.

Chapter 1: Basic Van Cleanliness

We should all acknowledge that a van is not going to be an antiseptic vacuum. If you have the windows or doors open even for a millisecond, the wind can blow in dust, pollen, leaves, or tiny insects. Unless you are camping on the production floor for a major cleaning product company, there will be a dusting of the outdoors in your van at all times. If you can write your name in the sand on the dashboard, it might be time to make a few adjustments!

First, consider bugs. Most of the insects and arachnids you meet along the way have an important job to do within their natural ecosystem. They also love getting a free ride with an all-you-can-eat buffet. More relevant to the matter at hand, they can bring with them some really unpleasant diseases, such as Lyme disease from ticks, or West Nile Virus and Zika from mosquitoes.

Make sure your screens and filters are all in good shape at all times, and that any free-standing screens fit tightly against your windows. If you use mosquito netting around your bed or sleeping areas, make sure there aren't any gaping holes, and repair or replace them as needed.

Check your entire food supply regularly for any invaders. In my experience, there is no such thing as "just one fly." So, make sure you're looking in the bins, the cupboards, the cooler, and the refrigerator daily to ensure no one is getting a free meal or reproducing in your important nutrients.

If you do find signs of unwanted arthropodic company, my first recommendation is to isolate the affected item or items. If you can wrap it in a grocery bag and drop it off in a trash can at a gas station or rest stop, all the better. If the infestation is in a larger object, such as a mattress or pillow, the first thing to do is isolate the source. Get the object out of the van, and wrap it in plastic- for example, those huge mattress moving bags can be really helpful in situations like this. I won't go so far as to recommend you carry one with you at all times, but keep this in mind as a "just in case" scenario.

Treatment of an infestation depends entirely on the type of insect involved and how far you're personally willing to go to get involved with this battle. Sometimes you can treat the object with commercially available chemicals and move on; other bugs require a greater level of finesse. I will say that if you decide to take matters into your own hands, remember first the impact of what you're doing to the area around you, the native wildlife, and your own family or travel companions. Letting off a flea bomb in the skoolie might make sense on paper, but where are the fumes going to go? Where are you going to do this so that it doesn't have a negative impact on land, air, water, or other wildlife? Don't say "the parking lot of the Wal-Mart where I buy the bomb," because that is the sort of thing that will go viral on social media in milliseconds. Insect infestations are very inconvenient and definitely have a very high "yuck" factor, but you can't have knee-jerk reactions when you live in a van. Be deliberate and plan carefully.

One way to mitigate potential insect problems is to keep all of your van surfaces as clean as possible. That means wiping down any counters or shelves, sweeping the floor, shaking out the bedding and rugs to rid them of any crumbs, and keeping up with all of your dishes.

Possibly the easiest way to incorporate this type of complete cleaning overhaul into your day is to make it part of the evening meal routine. After finishing supper, immediately wash and dry your dishes and store them back in their tote, cupboard, or drawer. If you have a sink, wash it out. Wipe down all of the counters or table tops, and use a hand broom to get the crumbs off of any indoor seating. Some people feel fine with doing a thorough sweep of the floor before closing up, but I personally prefer to do a quick mopping. Since the floor space in my van measures about 4 feet by three feet, this does not require exceptional effort- I can use a designated floor sponge and the leftover dish water. So long as there's nothing really gross or stinky floating in there, I can simply lean into the van through the door to quickly wipe down the floor.

Bedding can be tricky, depending on your rig's setup. If you're able to, remove linens from your bed each day and give them a good air fluff.

That should give you enough of a chance to disturb anything attempting to nest in it and allow you to inspect it for holes and swarms. I know this sounds terrible, but in your attempt to integrate with nature, nature will often make the first move.

Though it may be very tempting, do not spray bug spray inside the cabin, and especially not on your bedding. Most bug sprays stick to the skin via an oil base, so not only will they leave greasy streaks on your surfaces, but dirt and dust will also adhere to these sticky spots, giving you an equally bad time. There are some natural ways to dissuade insects from joining you on the road, such as vinegar, garlic, and citronella-based products. Just make sure you can live with the smell, and that storing your solution isn't more of a pain than a few irritating insects!

Chapter 2: Laundry Day!

When I asked my van buddies the number one thing they forget about when it came to chores and tidiness, almost all of them answered with "laundry day." At home, it's generally pretty easy to toss your dirty socks and tees in a hamper or dark corner and forget about them for a week or so. In a van, you probably have two days maximum before the socks in the corner start to haunt you, depending on the weather.

Hand-in-hand with keeping the van clean is coming up with an appropriate way to manage your laundry. This can be extra important when you're out-doors for long periods of time, as the pollen and dirt you encounter out there can easily trek into the van with you. Plus, sweat is one of those stenches that gets more pungent with time.

How you choose to do your laundry is entirely up to you. Some people like the convenience of stopping at a laundromat every so often. There are plenty of upsides to this plan. Many laundromats sell single-use detergent packets, which means you don't have to haul a bulky potential leak hazard around with you. Many laundromats also have amenities that we miss on the road such as running water, cold drink machines, air conditioning, and free WiFi. If your van is missing any of these, it might be a fine idea to spend a few hours basking in civilization in a laundromat.

Others prefer to go boondocking and stay boondocking. You can absolutely do your laundry from your van, as long as you have enough water for washing and rinsing. Roof racks are a fantastic place to let your clean clothes naturally air dry too; just make sure you firmly weigh your clothing down. Otherwise, you'll find yourself chasing your unmentionables through the wilderness as they dry and catch the wind.

If you choose to do your laundry from the van, I strongly urge you to be cautious about the type of detergent you use. The suds you dump onto the ground will be shared with all the flora and fauna in the area, so it's important to choose products that are non-toxic and environmentally friendly. The same goes for all of your cleaning products, shampoos, and soaps. Look for words like "biodegradable" on the labels, or check out a few tutorials online for making your own nature-friendly cleaning products. Don't worry, there are a few helpful links on this topic in the Resources section!

Chapter 3: Clean Van, Clean You

Now that I've gently eased you into the topic of basic van cleanliness, let's touch for a moment on personal hygiene.

On one hand, what does it matter what you smell like, or what kind of funk dwells deep within your armpits? You're alone or with your closest mates in the middle of nowhere, so is it important?

Well, yes and no. If you choose to take dirt baths and let your hair go completely *au naturel*, that is completely your prerogative. No judgment here. However, I will ask you to consider sponging up before and after you hit civilization.

You see, dirt itself is actually pretty harmless, compared to all the gross stuff humans spread around with their hands, their feet, and even with involuntary acts like breathing, yawning, sneezing, and coughing. When you touch something, all of the microscopic stuff living on that particular surface uses your body as a free ride. If you have an open wound, then touch your face, those microscopic particles use the opportunity to take a tour of your body.

Most of the stuff we touch is no big deal. Even if it isn't, our bodies are designed to fight off infections. Your immune system is equipped with natural warriors in the form of white blood cells, antibodies, mucus, and more to attack the invading virus, bacteria, fungus, or other toxins. Antibodies are produced as a reaction to acquired defense, so the first time your body encounters a particular germ, it may react poorly.

Want an easy way to prevent infection? Wash your hands. That may sound really familiar, but it bears repeating. Washing your body also gives you the opportunity to rid your skin of the bacteria, oils, and dead skin cells that are constantly piling up. Normally, that's no big deal, because your body is designed to take care of itself. But if you fall on a trail and scrape your knee, that bacteria is right there, ready to jump in and make a ruckus of your immune system. Don't let it. At the very minimum, keep wounds and compromised areas clean while your body does its job healing.

Furthermore, be mindful of what you track back into the van. When your skin and hair have more oil build up than usual, it's easy for germs and dirt to cling to your body and hitch a ride in your van. Again, that's rarely a big deal - except for when you're mingling with other people or environments.

Take, for example, White-Nose Syndrome, caused by a fungus that en-joys cold, damp, dark areas. White-Nose Syndrome affects hibernating bats. You may be wondering what that has to do with your human, van-life bathing habits. It's all about travel! White-Nose Syndrome has killed millions of bats since it was first identified in 2006, and it is theorized that it is spread minimally by bats travelling from cave system to cave system. Instead, it's largely spread by humans walking through cave systems, getting spores and guano on their shoes, and then walking in those shoes through another bat population, spreading the dangerous spores.

To mitigate the issue and keep the delicate ecosystem of caves in balance, many cave systems have installed disinfecting mats at the entrances and/or exits of their tour areas.

Similar logic applies to you, your natural biology, and the places you visit. The hiker's creed is "take nothing but photos; leave nothing but footprints," keep that in mind with your own personal hygiene and your interaction with local populations.

In the same line of thought, brushing your teeth in a van can be challenging without running water. It's a highly recommended activity for maintaining the health of your teeth and gums, and preventing infection originating in the mouth. You'll likely want to take care of your teeth when you're far from a dentist.

One suggestion is to keep a separate water bottle for clean water and rinse water. Rinse water can be captured in a tub and disposed of at any public restroom with a regular septic system. It's a bit more low-tech than a grey water system, but easy enough since brushing your teeth generally doesn't require a lot of water. You may wish to replace your toothbrush more frequently, or as many intrepid boondockers do, boil it from time to time, since the amount of rinsing you'll be able to do without running water is somewhat limited. I can't speak for the actual efficacy of boiling your toothbrush in the woods, so I'll leave that decision entirely up to you!

What about floss, and mouthwash? Absolutely wonderful consider-ations when it comes to maintaining dental hygiene, but not exactly environmentally friendly. Floss, for example, should absolutely not be discarded anywhere in the wild, as it can be harmful to wildlife. Instead, I recommend wrapping used floss in a bit of napkin and adding it to your regular trash. As long as you dispose of your trash frequently, it shouldn't create a noticeable stench.

Mouthwash is tricky, because you definitely don't want to accidentally re-use that. If you have a way to deposit your used swishes in the black water, that's ideal. If you choose to only use potent mouthwash when you're in a public bathroom, that's another great option. If you need to use a regular mouth-wash - either medicated or at a doctor's recommendation - the most important thing is that you don't accidentally introduce it to ground water or make it available to wildlife. This may mean carting around a well-labeled spitoon of sorts for the time being. Just be sure to dump, rinse, and sanitize it regularly to avoid creating a small, portable biohazard of your own!

I'm going to great pains here to avoid inadvertently shaming anyone's personal hygiene routine; however, I did want to include the topic to pro-vide tips to those who haven't considered the potential challenges. Many new van lifers don't think about the possible complications of try-ing to brush your teeth without running water, in the dark, while coyotes howl somewhere much closer than you would prefer. I bring these topics up simply to give those who are new to van life- or at least boondocking - some helpful ideas. Also, I want to remind those who have lost that sense of naivete through experience that cleanliness is still an important aspect of overall wellness!

Section 5: Mental Health Matters

Most of us turn to van life because there is something about stationary dwelling that just isn't "doing it" for us. Sometimes, there are unignorable mental health aspects at play that help drive our decision.

Perhaps the whole home/work routine isn't working. Maybe you feel life is passing you by too quickly. There might be high levels of anxiety caused by doing the same thing, every day. Maybe the reason you chose van life is because you needed to be outside with every bit of your soul, and let's be honest – you've sacrificed a lot to make your soul happy.

So, when you wake up in your beautiful van, to a 360-degree vista of exotic beauty, doing exactly what you want to be doing, how can you possibly feel depressed or anxious? If you're reading this book from the comfort of a house, apartment, condo, or other permanent dwelling, this idea may not make sense. For those who have been on the road for a bit, you've probably already experienced symptoms of road fatigue, anxiety, and depression, all related to the huge change you've just made in your life.

I have good news: you're absolutely not the first and only person who has ever felt this way. On the other hand, I have not-so-great news: these feelings don't just "go away."

In this section, I'll take a look at some common mental health issues that may pop up on the road. Even if you have never suffered from mental illness in the past, you are still human. Humans have emotions, and our minds and bodies respond to stress in ways that will never cease to shock and amaze us – even good stress! I fully hope everyone reading this book has a safe, enjoyable adventure, but if you do feel like something is not quite right on a mental or emotional level, this section is for you.

Please know that mental health is just as important as physical health and can even impact your immune response, sleep patterns, energy levels, and more. Do not ignore any changes in your thought patterns or emotions.

As mentioned before, this book is not intended to take the place of your regular therapist or counselor, and the advice of your professional team should always take priority!

NOTE:

- If you are currently in a decent place with your mental health and ready to read more about potential mental health challenges when you're on the road, go ahead and read on.

- If you may be triggered by reading about mental health right now, go ahead and jump to Section 6. I promise I'm not offended. Come back to this section when you're in a better space, and look after your own safety right now.

-

- If you are in crisis and may be a danger to yourself or others, or have a plan to cause harm, please put the book down and reach out for help. There is no shame in asking for help when you need it. If you can't get in touch with an understanding friend or family member right now, visit https://suicidepreventionlifeline.org/, or call the Lifeline at 1-800-273-8255.

When you're ready, read on to learn more about some of the unique challenges van living can have on our brains and how to keep your chin up and your outlook positive while dealing with them.

Chapter 1: The Reality of Road Fatigue

There are different types of discomfort that fall under the umbrella term of "road fatigue." Sometimes it's that zombie-like feeling you have when you've completed a long day of endless driving. You might be physically stiff, extremely sleepy, and devoid of thought or feeling. You even see headlights when you close your eyes!

Generally speaking, this level of fatigue will wear off quickly once you've had some rest, mental stimulation, or a nutritious meal. The symptoms you experience are simply the brain's way of saying that it's overloaded with the same stimuli, and it's time to switch things up a bit.

But What If It's Worse Than That?

The next level involves feeling stiff and sleepy, but you might be extra grumpy, too. Nothing sounds "good," and you're kind of mad about it. You can hear yourself whining like an overtired child, and you're actively embarrassed for anyone who's putting up with you right now. Still, you can't stop feeling irritated, even after a long rest or a break. Even when nothing particularly stressful is happening in the moment, you might find yourself thinking about something that made you feel cranky not too long ago, just to have a good reason for feeling the way you do.

If you're feeling this way right now, try this exercise:

1. Close your eyes (not while driving!)
2. Take several deep, cleansing breaths until you no longer feel actively cranky. Feeling tense is fine – that's an improvement.
3. Can you think of a time when you felt like this, even just a little bit? Maybe it was in school, when you had a whole bunch of things due all at once, and your friends were being weird, and your family was on your case about making a life for yourself. Perhaps it was at work, when it felt like literally everyone was in your face about some-thing you had to do NOW, NOW, NOW! It could have been in con-junction with getting prepared for a big holiday gathering or a huge vacation.
4. Don't replay that memory too much. Instead, fast forward to the part where you felt better. Chances are good that there was some event or date that occurred, after which all the pressure let up and you could go back to your normal levels of stress. Once the pressure released, so did all the negative feelings, right?

Now, open your eyes. In the next three minutes, you're going to get really grumpy again, because you'll realize you don't have any magic date or event that will cause you to feel less stressed out, and how can you possibly relax when you don't even know where you're going to find your next meal?

This may not make sense right now, but this is actually really good news. You're admitting that you're stressed out. Transitioning to van life is stressful. Even if you are fully physically prepared, your brain may not have gotten the memo.

There is a specific type of stress that occurs when you abruptly change routine on yourself. Think about how hard it is to start waking up an hour earlier every day. Then look around you. You have taken everything you've known, for your entire life, and put it in the rearview mirror. There are no bubble baths. There is no pizza delivery. You have probably gotten pretty good at going to the bathroom outside in the dark. This is not your normal!

This level of stress has been building and building. And just like everything else in this world, your emotional threshold for pressure can only bend so much before something has to give.

I actually had this epiphany while watching Old Faithful erupt at Yellowstone National Park. If you haven't been, I highly recommend it. Geysers erupt due to the relentless building pressure of steam released from water boiling far underground. When the pressure becomes too high, fountains of boiling water burst through the ground with incredible force. As the water cools below the boiling point, the eruption stops, and everything goes back to a calm, quiet state.

You are very much like a geyser, only less boiling water, and more complicated emotions. Your mind can handle stress. It accepts it as a reality. Logically, you know what's coming and probably have a good idea of how you'll react. When things go slightly sideways as you start your van adventure, you brush them off. It's no big deal. This is what you wanted. When you find yourself staring at the ceiling of the van at midnight, wishing you could talk to your best friend, you tell yourself you're doing something so much better. Squelch the feeling, and go to sleep. You chose to leave them behind, after all. This is not a healthy model to follow, and builds the pressure under your emotional geyser.

Stress can take a really heavy toll on your mental and emotional health. Stop trying to talk yourself out of your emotions. You're allowed to miss your friends. It makes perfect sense that you want to go home. Our brains and bodies thrive on routine, even if we don't agree with the concept. Yes, you wanted to do this. Yes, it was the best idea for you. But don't fool yourself that you should be proud and happy "instead of" mopey. It is not "failure" if you aren't feeling as much van life gusto on the third month as you did on the third day.

If you find yourself feeling grumpy, cranky, crunchy, indecisive, anti-social, or extra moody in any way, assess your honest stress level. What you need to do is simultaneously let yourself have feelings and find ways to direct that negative energy into something that will benefit you. Start with the exercise I've outlined. Maybe you don't have a date or event that will release this pressure, but you can create one.

Cry because you miss your friends. Then schedule a video call with as many of them as possible. Look at your itinerary and find the best time to go visit them. You have wheels – use them!

Miss lying in bed and watching television? Find a decent, inexpensive hotel for the night. Brad and I were able to score a fabulous hotel room in New Mexico for less than what camping spots in the area cost. Was it a penthouse suite? No, but it was clean, the sheets were cool, the air conditioning and the shower worked, and I actually cried because I saw a commercial on television for the first time in three months.

Your mind gives you plenty of red flags when the pressure starts to build, and since there is no shame in listening to what your body needs, pay attention to these signals. The final step in the exercise outlined earlier is to close your eyes again, and ask yourself honestly, what do you need? A break? A hug? A meal that reminds you of home? Once you've identified what you need to help you cope with the pressure you're feeling, set a course to make it happen. Chances are likely that you'll soon discover that things like spilling water on your seats will stop sending you into a tantrum.

The Side Effects of Having Too Much Time to Think
There's also a type of road fatigue that I call "The Backdoor Panics." That is in no way a medical term, but the best way I can describe the sensation.

At some point in your life, you've probably experienced this scenario. You're fast asleep. Suddenly, you wake up. Your pets might have made noise, you had to go to the bathroom, or you discovered your sleeping position was giving you a cramp. Either way, it was completely involuntary. You make all the necessary adjustments again, and before your head can hit the pillow, the Backdoor Panic appears. Out of nowhere, you remember the second grade science fair. Specifically, you remember how you forgot the science fair, because you thought it was still a week away. Chaos ensued, and you ended up with some half-cooked "project" accompanied by stammering and stuttering your way through a moment of epic failure. Suddenly, you've gone from a pleasant, restful state, to heart-racing, cold-sweating, full-blown anxiety!

Maybe it wasn't your second grade science fair, though this is a true story from my own past. I share this as an example of a real Back Door Panic I had somewhere on the road in Texas. I happened to see a mouse skeleton, which reminded me of the skeletons I used to collect as a kid, which started in second grade, and, well, you can see where this is headed. Regardless, this is not the sort of thing that should be keeping anyone awake at night. It's over. It's done. If it was the cataclysmic event that set off the rest of our collective destiny, there's still nothing that can be done about it, especially not in the middle of the night.

But this is exactly how the Back Door Panic works. It shows up when your mind is relaxed, and you have nothing but empty hours to dwell on all sorts of terrible things.

What does this have to do with van living? When you live in a van, you will have plenty of quiet, empty time to fill with thoughts. When you're feeling particularly stressed or vulnerable, your brain will tenderly associate all of the times you felt lousy, and run it past you in a never-ending loop of failure. Basically, your bad feelings come in through the "backdoor" of your mind, and as a result, you may start to feel super depressed or unbelievably anxious.

The fact that a complete stranger is explaining this phenomenon to you should give you hope that you are not alone. Even if you're feeling pretty great about everything, those long stretches on the road can be very tricky for the mind. I strongly recommend preparing adequate distractions, such as music, podcasts, audio books – anything to keep you less focused on the dark recesses of your memory.

If you're not in the driver's seat, you have even more options available. As long as you have a way to keep your phone charged, indulge in some phone games. If you're feeling lonely, hit up some forums or social media groups in a niche you love. As a word of caution, though, don't forget that social media groups can sometimes be incredibly volatile. If you're feeling particularly vulnerable, back away from any outlet, group, or post that is making you feel stressed and explosive. Don't let someone else's mindless words trigger your emotional state. If it's too late and the damage is done, my best recommendation is to reach out to someone sympathetic, such as a friend who also shares your interests.

For those who are travelling in pairs or as a family, I encourage you to be open with your traveling companions about how you're feeling. Even a skoolie is a very small, contained area, and your change in attitude and mood will be noticed. By communicating your feelings, you'll prevent a chain reaction of discontent, unease, and even paranoia. Plus, there's something about sharing your negative emotions that seems to defuse them a bit.

Success is not measured by how many consecutive nights you stay in your van. Your self-worth is not determined by how many meals you've eaten by yourself in the woods. Snuggling down in a hotel room with a delivery pizza isn't a sign of weakness or failure. Instead, these are signs that your mind needs a break, and that you are honoring that need. While it would be great if we could all just handle infinite amounts of stress without cracking, that is not reality. Honor your signs of stress and anxiety, and take care of them before you become a full geyser.

Chapter 2: Finding and Continuing Mental Health Care on the Road

For some reason, therapy and counseling have gotten a bad reputation as an act of desperation or failure. Honestly, I don't understand this concept. If you've ever been to a Happy Hour event with your coworkers and complained about your boss, if you've talked to your spouse about a friend who is getting on your nerves, or if you've sat with a best friend over a cup of coffee and spilled all of your secrets... you have essentially completed the steps required for a therapy session.

The point of therapy and counseling is to talk through your issues with someone who is qualified to help guide your train of thoughts to help you focus on potential solutions, changes, or coping mechanisms. That's it. A therapist will not "cure you," but they will ease the burden of stress and pressure. A weekly or monthly session is usually the perfect opportunity to vent all of your frustrations while an empathetic therapist or counselor helps you dive into why you're frustrated, what caused you to react negatively, and come up with some ways to deal with your emotions.

When you're on the road, however, you can't just pop into your therapist's office once a week. If you've been in therapy for awhile, you'll know that freshly gutted feeling that comes with knowing you'll have to take your mental health into your own hands. Thankfully, technology has made it so that we can continue getting the help we need, even when we're on the road.

If one-on-one sessions are your jam, then consider online therapy options. You can choose from video conferencing, texting, emailing, and even phone calls with your designated therapist. Some programs allow for any-time-contact and assistance, while others offer flexible scheduling. This means that as long as you have a smartphone or other workable device and a clear signal, you can connect with a trained professional who can help you talk it out.

If you absolutely love the care professionals you have now, it can't hurt to approach them about telehealth. Before the COVID-19 outbreak of 2020, this was an almost unheard-of practice. However, with in-person visits limited due to potential spread of disease, more and more established practices are open to contacting patients through video calls.

You may prefer more interactive group sessions instead. It can be very helpful to talk through your concerns in a room full of sympathetic, like-minded individuals who have had similar experiences. You may think that hitting the road means leaving group sessions behind, but you'll be surprised to find that many cities, towns, and even villages have meetings that anyone is welcome to attend.

Granted, if you have anxiety about new social settings, you might not feel very cavalier about walking into a room full of complete strangers and airing all of your deepest secrets. If that sounds like the last possible thing you might ever want to do, take heart- online virtual group sessions exist for exactly this reason.

You might be a little concerned about the privacy aspect, especially if you're sitting in a van with the windows down, trying to be heard over a dubious phone connection. For that reason, I recommend doing a little scouting before you join in. Some of the best online support groups will have not just meetings, but also a forum or group page on social media where you can chat with others in the group and get to know each other. The pressure is minimal. If you don't like it, then unsubscribe, unfollow, block, delete, or whatever combination of words that particular forum uses to leave that group. There are thousands of communities out there if you're willing to do the legwork to find a group that most fits your needs.

Having a support system on the road is crucial for anyone who might be feeling extra stress, anxiety, or depression related to the massive life changes related to leaving "home" behind in favor of van life. While not every person who cares about you will understand why you're on the road, nearly everyone will appreciate how much change can impact our emotional and mental health. You need someone in your corner who is willing to listen, guide, and instigate coping or change – whichever is needed to help you find a healthier outlook to your stressors.

Chapter 3: When It Becomes Too Much

There may be a time when you start to feel a certain way. If you were still living in a house with a 9-5 job, you'd say you were feeling burnt out, and that you needed a vacation. But here you are, living in a van, essentially living an eternal vacation. How can you possibly be burnt out?

As I've mentioned repeatedly, van life is stressful. On top of that, regular stress doesn't end just because you don't have a mailbox and a driveway. You may not have to deal with your daily commute, but traffic is still a reality. You don't have to appear in an office, but income is still helpful. You won't have to come face-to-face with that annoying relative, but chances are good that they still remember your phone number. Stress is everywhere, and for all of us, sometimes too much is just *way too much*.

When this happens, take a reverse vacation. Go hunker down with some friends or family members you love. You'll be surprised at how cool people feel with your van parked in their driveway. (On a related note – if you have a skoolie, you might need to make parking arrangements before you try parking in a suburban housing development!) A few days of indoor plumbing, climate control, cable television, and a microwave might be what your soul is craving in order to feel like balance is restored.

Alternately, you can tap out and plant for a bit. This means going deep into a boondocking area, where there's no phone signal, no WiFi, no people. It's just you, nature, and your van. The first time you do this, you may want to prepare beforehand by stopping at a grocery store, making sure you've got plenty of ice and clean clothes, and ensuring your spare tire and Med Prep and repair kits are all good to go.

Once you've got all the necessities, find the most intimidating camping spot you can find and hang out there for a few days. Meditate. Journal. Read. Draw. Create. Hike. Whatever brings you solace and serenity and keeps your mind from spiraling in on itself – this is the time to do it.

On the entirely opposite side of the coin, maybe you need the rush of city life. If you've been living in a metropolitan area your entire life, and you've just spent two months boondocking, the solitude might be causing you stress. If the funds are available, put the van in long-term parking, and have a city adventure.

I will fully admit that I have done this. After spending weeks in the deserts of the American West, Brad and I decided we needed a change of pace, so we booked a trip to Hawaii. We stayed in a hotel, rotted on the beach, ordered room service, and did a whole bunch of super-touristy things that we would usually laugh at. But it worked. When we came back to the van, we weren't upset at all about the sand in our pants. We didn't mind that weird soup smell that would never go away. We felt more prepared for deeper boondocking because we saw the city lights and felt that much more comfortable with the stars for having done so.

Van life is not a black-and-white sort of adventure. You can come and go. You can stop and rest, or keep moving. The whole point of van life is to custom tailor your daily experience to feed your soul, which includes your mind and your emotions. There's no such thing as "cheating" or "failing." Do whatever you need to do to keep yourself healthy and fulfilled to live your very best van life.

Health and Wellness in 2020: Special Notes About COVID-19 Considerations

I started planning this book long before the COVID-19 pandemic was on the world's collective radar. When I first started making notes, I included all of the bits about being careful to not pick up and spread strange diseases due to being a traveler. I had no idea what was in store with a global pandemic on the horizon.

When I hit the road in 2018, I was startled by how often I got the sniffles or a little sore throat. Was it allergies? Was it related to incredibly different climates to my muggy and volatile Ohio weather? Or was I coming down with a swift bug? Without a full medical laboratory and an advanced degree in medicine, I had no way of knowing. So, I did what I could to boost my immune system with good nutrition, exercise, and sleep. I also kept the van clean, and practiced a reasonable amount of hand-washing. We had disinfectant wipes in the van for any questionable moments and hand sanitizer at the ready. At the same time, Brad and I thought nothing of taking our toothbrush into a rest station or fast food restaurant to clean up quickly with some running water. There were no masks and we regularly visited heavily congested parks and museums.

The current COVID-19 landscape is much different. Reservations are required to get into National Parks and museums – if they're even open at all. Camping in organized sites is extremely limited, and those that do have bathrooms may no longer allow access to them. In some states, restaurants are open for take-out only and you must patiently wait in line for the chance to enter a grocery store.

In some ways, van life is less stressful. Everything we need is artfully contained within a single space. Hardly anyone touches our surfaces except us, and self-quarantine is pretty much our way of life.

In other ways, living in a van can be much more stressful. Entertainment options run out quickly. Spontaneous travel to new locations is limited, as reservations to enter parks and campsites often sell out months in advance.

Travelling between states is, in several cases, prohibited. Attractions you've been eager to visit may be closed, and nearly every public event has been cancelled or very strictly limited.

Thankfully, one thing that has not been cancelled is nature. The trees are still growing, the winds are still blowing, and the flowers are still blooming. As I'm writing this section, the West Coast is currently on fire, and the East Coast is getting pummeled by hurricanes. So, that phrase might be slightly tinged with shades of hope, but until the actual end of the planet, nature is not officially done.

Before you set out each day, I do recommend taking a look at travel advisories to see where you're permitted to go based on your most recent location. I understand that no one wants to purposefully spread disease. I further understand that van lifers are, by nature, a rebellious sort. Different states have different requirements and penalties for not obeying their travel requirements. If you have the choice to go anywhere you want, choose a place where the risk is less. Quite frankly, every van lifer should be exquisitely prepared to quarantine in their van for fourteen days!

There's a little phrase that sticks in my mind at times like this: Calculated Risk. There are a lot of contagious diseases out there, and that's why we should all be exercising a significant amount of caution. This is especially so if we have a lifestyle in which we meet and share space with a lot of different people in rapid succession. Van dwellers should already be washing their hands thoroughly and using hand sanitizer frequently.

When Brad and I first hit the road in 2018, we each had a pocket-sized hand sanitizer on our person at all times, plus a container of sanitizing wipes in the back. Neither of us are anywhere near the stereotype of "germaphobes," either. I grew up riding horses and his family had a sheep farm. We're simply aware that gross stuff can get on your hands, and rather than getting it in your mouth or where you sleep, it's best to clean it off.

Masks are difficult. I get it. I'm constantly running into things because I can't see over the edges, sweating under them, and fidgeting under them. They're not something I love, but something I deal with because they let me do what I love, like visit breweries and try new foods. Again, always with calculated risk. Brad and I tend to visit places at non-peak times, request to sit in very low-traffic areas, and get take-out whenever possible. Sharing a growler of ale and a woodfired pizza in the back of the van while camped for the night is an absolute ideal type of evening for me, and totally worth wearing a mask to make it all happen.

Really, many van folks are already social distancing champions. We live a sort of lifestyle in which not being able to see what nearby campers are up to is actually a treat. I remember finding this prime boondocking location in Arizona – it was just us, a single tree, and the sunset. And then an RV rolled up. "Oh, come ON!" Brad lamented into the sunset. "How did you even find us?" That's the sort of attitude I've found prevalent amongst many van lifers. We've got a hearty sense of community, but if we wanted to hang out with people all the time, we would've stayed in the suburbs.

Therefore, in the name of calculated risk, I encourage you to hang on to your van lifer ideals. Yes, life was much more interesting when we could stop and talk to everyone we encountered on the trails. You still can ask the locals the best places to check out. From a distance of 6 feet, of course, and while wearing a mask. You might think these are paranoia-fueled rules, but basic outdoorsmanship and survival skills are rooted in taking precautions that mutually benefit you and nature. If you can run your backpack up a tree to discourage night predators from stopping by for a snack, you can also slip a mask on before interacting with people face-to-face.

And then, when you've reached the apex of an incredible hike, or found that boondocking spot where no one can find you, you can slip off your mask, take several deep breaths, and absolutely revel in the delicious moments of being a nature-loving, solitude-seeking van lifer.

Conclusion

At the very beginning of this book, I promised you that there wouldn't be any overwhelming revelations, and I hope that remains true. My goal in writing this book was to remove some of the surprises and stigma, and provide a whole heap of reminders and tips for staying healthy while you're on the road.

For our inaugural van trip, Brad and I started out in late April. We had a great run until September, when it seemed like we were getting hit with back-to-back colds. At first, we were terribly stubborn and tried to push through, but that was a very, very bad idea in retrospect. If we had paused until we were feeling better, we could have easily extended our trip and really enjoyed the opportunities that were just beyond the doors of the van. Instead, we ended up crawling back to home base in mid-October, worn out, and carrying an impressive-but-unnecessary array of cold medicines and throat lozenges.

Is this a cautionary tale? Not entirely. I can't stop you from picking up minor illnesses, and I'm literally the last person who can prevent you from getting injured. I don't want you to give up your dreams, and I definitely think you should go base-jumping if that's your life's dream. I want you to exercise caution, but I want you to have fun in your feral new lifestyle, after all!

What I'm hoping this book does is open your eyes to a little bit of the reality that is van life. The models on social media make it look so clean and airy, beautiful and decadent. The "beautiful" part is accurate. "Airy" can be, too, if the weather is nice. But clean? Decadent? Those parts are entirely up to you, and in my opinion, are also mutually exclusive.

I encourage each person reading this book to take care of yourself, whether that means following the recommendations and tips presented in this book to the letter, or just paying attention to the cues your body is feeding you. I want you to know that if you are feeling a certain type of bad – whether that's in your body, in your mind, or in your emotions – there are things you can do to help yourself feel a little better.

If you haven't experienced life on the road yet, you might find many of these tips to be common sense and basic knowledge. Before you roll your eyes and leave a scathing review on Amazon, consider how you will react the first time you experience the pains of food poisoning... at midnight, during a thunderstorm, in the middle of a National Forest, with no toilet and three napkins. At that moment, you will be questioning all of the decisions that got you to this moment, and wondering what you could have done differently to avoid this very situation. It is from the perspective of that person, and for that person, that I wrote this book. Just a few years ago, that person was me, and I was hideously unprepared for the adventure to which I had committed myself.

Perfection is impossible, and disease is inevitable. However, by exercising calculated risk, and doing our best for ourselves, by ourselves, we can ride this van life adventure for as long as we wish. I wrote extensively about knowing how to be able to fix your van in my first book, *How to Live the Dream: Things Every Van Lifer Needs to Know.* The same concepts apply here, with your body and your mind.

I've kicked around what it means to be "successful" at van life, and at the end of the day, I think it boils down to this:

- Are you doing well? Mentally, physically, emotionally?
- Is the van still running?
- Do you have enough of what you need to survive?
- Are your emotional needs met?
- Do you wake up every morning feeling pretty good about your van life?

If you can answer yes to these questions on most days, then I'd say you're pretty successful. Congratulations, and here's to many happy travels in your van life!

Resources

I like to include resources at the end of each of my books, because I love learning. I figure if you picked up a book with "How To..." in the title, chances are good that you love learning too. I don't actually know everything about everything, but I do a lot of research to write these books, which involves immeasurable time spent searching for reliable, current sources and effort reaching out to my van life buddies to learn about their experiences, as well.

This book, however, is unique. While some of the following links will lead to resources where you can get more information about a particular topic, others are educational sites that can enrich your knowledge about the topics covered in each chapter. If you want camp burner recipes, I've got links. If you want a great YouTube video to help your children learn about how your immune system works, I've included those types of links as well. Don't worry, everything is labeled, and I didn't include anything gory or questionable.

Having struggled with a chronic condition myself, I feel like knowledge gives us power over things that we can't necessarily control, but can mitigate and learn to live with.

I am in no way affiliated with any of these links, nor is anyone I know. I was not paid or reimbursed in any way for referencing them. These are simply resources I found in my own independent research, gathered, and included here because I felt they may be of use to other van folks and prospective van folks. I have no control or input into what is published in these links, either.

What You Need to Know

These are all educational links, pulled from peer-reviewed, scientific sources. As I started to write this book, I realized that I have no credibility on medical topics. I pay attention, I read, and I do a ton of research.

These links may be only vaguely referenced in the text, but I wanted to "show my work" in spots, to demonstrate that I'm not just inventing this information. The following represent some of the sites I used extensively throughout the planning and writing of this book. If these articles aren't relevant to your situation, I encourage you to search these resources for more information.

Germs vs Surfaces:
- *How long do nosocomial pathogens persist on inanimate surfaces? A systematic review* https://www.ncbi.nlm.nih.gov/pmc/articles/PMC1564025/

Keeping clean:
- *Cleaning and Disinfection* https://www.cdc.gov/mrsa/community/environment/index.html

How Antibodies Work:
- *Antibodies* https://www.newscientist.com/term/antibodies/

An Interesting Article about Epidemiology:
- *How Europeans brought sickness to the New World* https://www.sciencemag.org/news/2015/06/how-europeans-brought-sickness-new-world

Preventive Care

Preventive care is a bit of a pet topic for me, so I was very excited to include a chapter that focused on the basics. I also know that everyone is different, and comes from a different background. You are welcome to disagree with my assessments regarding preventive care. I've included a few links here so you can gather the information needed to make your own informed decisions.

Medical Checkups:
- *www.Healthline.com "How Often Should You See Your Doctor for a CheckUp"*

https://www.healthline.com/health/how-often-should-you-get-routine-checkups-at-the-doctor#benefits

Oral health care:

- *Centers for Disease Control and Prevention "Oral Health Tips"* *https://www.cdc.gov/oralhealth/basics/adult-oral-health/tips.html*

Vaccinations and travel considerations:

- *https://www.vaccines.gov/who_and_when/travel*
- *https://wwwnc.cdc.gov/travel*
- *https://www.cdc.gov/rabies/transmission/index.html#:~:text=Rabies%20virus%20is%20transmitted%20through,bite%20of%20a%20rabid%20animal.*

Maintenance medications:

- *https://www.cdc.gov/nchs/fastats/drug-use-therapeutic.htm*

Insurance Considerations

My mantra through this entire section was "don't write an entire book about insurance." That's not why you're here. That being said, I know that healthcare costs in the United States are very, very high. I know that most people on the road aren't making a sweet six-figure paycheck each week, either. I wanted to provide substantial information on the topic, so you can make informed decisions about what makes the most sense for you, your family, and your overall financial situation.

Emergency Room vs. Urgent Care Details:

- *https://www.debt.org/medical/emergency-room-urgent-care-costs/*

Shopping for individual health care plans:
For this particular exercise, I didn't want to provide just one option or view, so here are a few different links that can provide guidance through searching for a healthcare plan outside of employer benefits.

- *How much Does Health Insurance Cost Per Month?* *https://www.* *healthmarkets.com/content/health-insurance-cost-per-month*
- *Online Healthcare Finder* *https://finder.healthcare.gov/*
- *Private Health Care Plans Outside Open Enrollment* *https://www.* *healthcare.gov/private-plan-exceptions-outside-open-enroll-* *ment/*
- *How to Buy Individual Health Care* *https://www.bcbsm.com/* *index/health-insurance-help/faqs/topics/buying-insurance/* *how-to-purchase-individual-health-insurance.html*
- *Guide to Buying an Individual Health Care Plan* *https://www.in-* *surance.com/health-insurance/health-insurance-basics/how-* *to-buy-an-individual-health-plan.html*

Food and Nutrition

All of these links lead to recipes and meal ideas. I can't vouch for how delicious, easy, or practical all of them are, because I used resources that included many ideas. I have tried many of them, and I feel pretty confident that there's at least one tasty, new meal option for you in at least one of these links! All of these are written with camping/boondocking in mind, which makes them particularly useful for those living the van life.

- *From "Van Life UK Survivors Guide":* *https://www.vanlifeuksurvi-* *vorsguide.co.uk/post/how-to-never-get-bored-cooking-with-* *a-single-gas-burner-or-camping-stove?fbclid=IwAR0KbqV-* *15nOJ4Io-geil17BNB_BCFIJKSHBT9RTYYMh4-BSDQEn61n06ypEk*
- *My favorite campfire pizza:* *https://www.freshoffthegrid.com/campfire-pizza-recipe/*
- *Fantastic Mac and Cheese* *https://www.foodnetwork.ca/cana-* *da-day/photos/one-pot-camping-recipes/#!campfire-mac-* *and-cheese*
- *From "Fresh Off The Grid"" *https://www.freshoffthegrid.com/* *camping-recipe-index/?fwp_activity=car-camping*
- *Food Network's Camping Hacks:* *https://www.foodnetwork.ca/*

fun-with-food/photos/easy-camping-food-hacks/

Exercise

Believe it or not, I've tried nearly all of these. I'm not going to tattle on myself as to which I didn't do, but I will confirm that at one point, I was doing burpees next to the van to determine what would make them any easier. Being that I'm not a huge fan of burpees, that's a pretty subjective topic, but rest assured that a significant amount of conscientious research went into this chapter.

If you're doing any of these for the first time, please pay attention to the directions and details to avoid injury. Never exercise against the advice of your medical team. Take it easy, and honor your body. Most of all, have fun moving!

- *Outdoor Yoga Guidance and Routines*
  https://www.yogajournal.com/practice/call-of-the-wild
  https://www.doyou.com/your-guide-to-outdoor-yoga/

- *Yoga for Travelers (from Yoga with Adriene):*
  https://www.youtube.com/watch?v=C0U7v4iCemM

Specific Yoga Poses:
- *Warrior Pose:* _https://www.mondaycampaigns.org/de-stress-monday/add-warior-yoga-pose-wellness-routine_
- *Extended Triangle Pose:*
  https://www.yogajournal.com/poses/extended-triangle-pose
- *Extended Side Angle Pose:*
  https://www.youtube.com/watch?v=0lfzG9jH6cM&app=desktop
  _https://www.instagram.com/p/BeZ0DDellwv/?utm_source=ig_share_sheet&igshid=ff45nb45b1gi_

HIIT and Body Weight Exercise Tips:
- _https://www.fitnessblender.com/videos/insane-hiit-chal-lenge-bodyweight-only-high-intensity-interval-training-work-out_

- https://www.shape.com/fitness/workouts/lose-fat-fast-hiit-bodyweight-workout
- https://www.nerdfitness.com/blog/how-to-stay-in-shape-while-traveling/

Specific Cardio Exercises:
- *High Knees:*
  https://classpass.com/movements/high-knees#:~:text=High%20Knees%20are%20a%20cardio,a%20wide%20variety%20of%20work-outs.
- *Squat Jumps:*
  https://www.youtube.com/watch?v=CVaEhXotL7M
- *Goblet Squats:*
  https://www.youtube.com/watch?v=MxsFDhcyFyE
- *Step-Ups:*
  https://www.youtube.com/watch?v=BeN9ZcYY5iM

Exercise and Wellness for Climbers and Hikers:
https://mountainmadness.com/resources/climbing-rating-systems
https://thetrek.co/8-best-stretches-thru-hikers/
https://jennybruso.com/unlikelyhikers/

Managing Chronic Conditions

I want to be as delicate and kind regarding various chronic conditions. All of them require a different level of maintenance, and each individual who lives with a chronic condition has their own experience. In my attempts to avoid making sweeping generalizations, I found that many resources do just that. From my own personal experiences, I am aware that living with Alzheimer's has different considerations than coping with cancer treatment, so I was pretty shocked to find that many sites just group every condition together.

The links that I've provided here provide some information about what chronic conditions are, and a few tips for managing them on the road. These tips seem to imply that people do not leave their home except in the face of disaster. The tips are solid for anyone who wishes to explore the world around them voluntarily, however.

A Definition of Chronic Conditions:
https://www.cms.gov/Research-Statistics-Data-and-Systems/Statistics-Trends-and-Reports/Chronic-Conditions/CC_Main

How to Manage Your Chronic Disease During a Disaster
https://www.cdc.gov/chronicdisease/about/manage/disaster.htm

Chronic Disease in Uncertain Times
https://newsinhealth.nih.gov/2020/08/chronic-disease-uncertain-times

Dealing with Emergencies

This is another information-rich topic that I could wax on about all day, especially given my penchant for falling. The following links will help you prepare for the possibility of an emergency, and lead to further resources that can provide more extensive training and details than I could possibly fit in this book!

- *When to go to the ER:* https://www.healthline.com/health/right-care-right-time/where-to-go#1
- *What to do in an emergency:* https://www.webmd.com/heart-disease/features/5-emergencies-do-you-know-what-to-do
- *A thorough, printable first aid guide from Simple Family Preparedness:* https://simplefamilypreparedness.com/first-aid-quick-guide/
- *REI's Expert Guide to first aid kits (this section of REI's site provides a significant amount of information for van dwellers!):* https://www.rei.com/learn/expert-advice/first-aid-checklist.html
- *Things to keep in mind in case YOU are involved in an emergency:* https://www.health.harvard.edu/staying-healthy/are-you-prepared-for-a-medical-emergency

Insect Management

You have a lot of options when it comes to taking care of the involuntary passengers you bring along on the trip. I consider this site a good introduction to the dilemma without forcing any potential ethical considerations. I know there are some humane and inhumane options when it comes to getting rid of pests, so I encourage you to work within your moral guidelines to keep infestations from happening.

https://www.boondockersbible.com/knowledgebase/how-to-keep-bugs-from-getting-into-your-rv/

Laundry Day

Here are a few sites and a video that can address the question of how to do your laundry on the road. From choosing bio-friendly products to the actual steps involved, this should help you keep your clothes clean and in good repair while you're on the road. (Or hit a laundromat, if this isn't your forte!)

https://thecampingnerd.com/laundry-boondocking/
https://greatist.com/health/27-chemical-free-products-diy-spring-cleaning
https://www.youtube.com/watch?v=gePt65DyW2g

The Immune System

With absolutely no disrespect intended, it has come to my attention that one can receive a significant amount of top-notch education and not know how the immune system works. There have been several times in my discussions with others that I have said, "but that's not how the immune system works," only to have to explain it. Not being a medical professional myself, I had to call in the experts for assistance. Hopefully, these links will help you as much as they have helped me.

https://www.ncbi.nlm.nih.gov/books/NBK279364
https://www.hopkinsmedicine.org/health/conditions-and-diseases/the-immune-system
https://www.youtube.com/watch?v=oqGuJhOeMek

Online Therapy

Mental health is so incredibly important. As I was writing this book, nearly everyone I reached out to asked me to make sure I included a section about mental health. It's something that is frequently overlooked, especially when you're supposed to be having the time of your life. Living on the road has its own unique challenges, and while the van life community is incredibly supportive, sometimes it's best to call in a professional! Here are a few links to online therapy resources, as referenced in the text.

- *Talk Space:* *https://www.talkspace.com/online-therapy/*
- *Better Help:* *https://www.betterhelp.com/start/*
- *A Comprehensive List of Options:* *https://www.verywellmind.com/best-online-therapy-4691206*

These are not links exclusively for those living in a van. Absolutely anyone can use these links, as well as the emergency mental health contacts I've included within the text. Being a modern human being is complicated, so please don't feel ashamed to take advantage of any resource that can help you make it through rough times.

COVID-19

We are absolutely bombarded with information about the COVID-19 pandemic of 2020, and hopefully, in the future, all of these links will be useless. For now, these are some frequently-updated sites that are helpful for travelers trying to make sense of van life rules and restrictions in an ever-changing landscape:

Tips for Travelers:
https://www.cdc.gov/coronavirus/2019-ncov/travelers/communication-resources.html
https://www.ustravel.org/toolkit/covid-19-resources-destinations
https://www.cnn.com/travel/article/us-state-travel-restrictions-covid-19/index.html

Reviews

Reviews and feedback help improve this book and the author. If you enjoy this book, we would greatly appreciate it if you could take a few moments to share your opinion and post a review on Amazon.

Also by Kristine Hudson

Things Every Lifer Needs to Know

mybook.to/vanlife

Finding Success Outside The Traditional Office

mybook.to/workfromanywhere

How to Choose the Ultimate Side-hustle

mybook.to/side-hustle

The Modern Woman's Guide to Living Wild and Free

mybook.to/vanbundle1

Living and Prospering Wherever You Wish

mybook.to/vanbundle2

Lightning Source UK Ltd.
Milton Keynes UK
UKHW020619060722
405448UK00001B/19